THE UPS AND DOWNS OF LIFE

KYRA HAYMON

EPIGRAPH

The cover picture is a seesaw and a picture of two trees. On the up side, the sun is out and the tree is flourishing, full of green leaves. On the down side, the moon is out and the tree has lost most of its leaves. The title is The Ups and Downs of Life.

This book is dedicated to all on the seesaw called life. As you go through life's cocoon of seasons, hopefully you will remember, changes happen on the inside.

Enjoy this journal of free verses, prose, songs, dreams, reflections, and inspirations. May it warm you to know, you are not alone.

CONTENTS

THE WOMB CHILD

In the womb I'm held tight and carried wherever I go; I have my own space to grow. Every day I come to absorb whether it's food or sounds; I take in what's around. I feed on it, every nugget, every bit.

Sometimes it's noisy and I feel pressure; yet, I don't know whether to be restless or content. Then comes this wonderful taste, it takes away the pressure, now I'm in a happy place. This is my crave, my all time fave.

Whatever my state from the items on my plate, I already have a taste in my mouth before leaving out.

CHILD OF INDEPENDENCE

You're the child of independence, running wild and free; your name is curiosity. Like a child taking his first footsteps, you feel free to roam. The open field is where you'll discover who you are and what you can do. As for where you came from, that's already a part of you.

Like a child leaving his home, you're no longer kept. Your strength is your shelter. Whatever you touch, you feel, out goes the fairy tales and the happily-ever-after.

CHILDHOOD LESSON

Some say love brought me into this world, that I don't know, but one day I was formed. Since then life has been one big adjustment! They say I'm free now to form my own identity, to pursue my dreams with the gifts within me! But who do I listen to in a world full of voices? Who will teach me not to limit my choices?

Ah, I shall draw from what my childhood taught me. One, develop immunity to things that get you down. Yes, my heart will be a prey to the bitter cold of reality, but it must grow immune to its effects. Two, choose words carefully, people will use them to see inside of you. My words are definitions, meanings, and painted images for one to see. Thirdly, playing with others is fun, but it can also leave bruises. Therefore be aware, some people will leave bruises as they come and go.

Hopefully love will teach me other lessons I should know.

THINGS ACCOMPLISHED WITHIN

Are there many things you want to do, but you don't have the strength? Does it feel as if someone drained you and left you to sink? Maybe some of the things you accomplished today were things you wanted to do. But the majority of the day was probably spent doing what others asked you to do.

'All day: yes, no, yes, no, what else do you want me to do?'

I guess I'll haul this heavy weight of mine until the night chores are through.

When you are blocked in, the only sound you hear are the noises surrounding you, and nothing else matters unless it's within your four walls. It's hard to even imagine life outside the four walls especially when your vision is limited to somewhere within. The only key to unlock the door is hoping for something more: use your imagination.

IS THIS LEGAL?

Is it because we're immigrants, we're treated this way? We work hard and we are faithful. Yet it's been weeks but still no pay.

It's not right but what can we say? We were hired because we're illegal immigrants, so we could be treated this way.

Is this legal? Is there anyone who will speak for us? Who will stand with us while we work to get the legal papers that can fight for us?

Until then, I would like to say, Jesus will hear us, when we all come together and pray.

CONFORM OR TRANSFORM

Conform, conform, and conform, early on we were taught to conform! Every citizen must fit in with society. Really, if we're in a Jungle for years, what kind of animal will we be? Tamed or untamed, it's still a beast. Everyone in the mirror might as well be looking at me.

Conform, conform, and conform, early on we were taught to conform! What happens when the lines between the tame and the untamed start to fade? Do we teach another lesson? Do we learn another trade? Do we fall back on tolerance when we have no answer for ignorance? Will we even recognize the norm after everyone conforms?

Conform, conform, and conform, early on we were taught to conform! Nobody is wrong, just free, being who they were meant to be! Everybody has their dream. Just show love, don't be mean! And when we say love, we mean tolerant; unless you are someone on the street, like an animal, in need of a free treat. You see, in the zoo, we feed the animals but here in the jungle everyone is dispensable. Conform, conform, and conform anybody out there feel the need to transform?

SEEING ONLY COLORS

Black, white, red, yellow and brown are the colors of this town. Everyone divides into their own groups. No one is exceptional; they just use one another to feel special. They tear, and poke, at one another for attention.

People use other people to illustrate what is, and what isn't, and what they aren't. Alone, no one has a voice. Yet at times I feel it's not by choice. It's as if everyone is bound. No one takes a stand to build uniqueness, and harmony. Everyone is blocked in this black, white, red, yellow and brown colored town, seeing only the colors, never the rainbow.

LOVE IS GIVING

Love is when the pleasure of giving is your greatest return.

Love is when your giving is received with thanks, not as something earned.

Love is when you give, and it's so pleasingly sought after, that it keeps you reaching to give more. However, when your love is not wanted, it can leave you feeling lonely.

Still, don't let the expectations of others push you to pretend. Learn to give, how and when.

WHAT MOMMA SAID MAKES YOU WISH

Mom said,
"Pray and ask the Lord for your husband.
Because if he isn't yours, he's somebody else's husband.
Love can bring heartache, when there's things on your shelf that belong to someone else."

MAKES YOU WISH

As if walking in the middle of a desert, nobody is to be found. As if in the woods, nature is the only sound.
Walking, wondering whether there's other life on earth. When will the end come? When will you find true rest?
Walking, stranded on a desert, on a desert that has no end . . . Makes you wonder, when did it begin? Makes you wonder, what is the word friend?
While walking in the woods, you see a bird flying free. Flying in the air, he calls another, but you're feeling all alone, makes you wish, makes you wonder.

I SAW ME

Thank you Lord for my upbringing. When you know better, you do better. I'm convinced people just need to be taught better. That's why I go out every day to tell others Jesus has a better way. Doing drugs, smoking, drinking messes with your mind and it can take you out before your time. Mom didn't like me going out every day talking to strangers alone. So Mom told my nephew to go with me when I leave home. There was no question, I was saved, more saved than Suzy Q!

This Sunday I decided to make it official. Sitting in the pews at church with my friends, the pastor's sermon was coming to an end. My god sister got up to be baptized, so I got up too. That's what people do to show their commitment is true. So I walked down the aisle and was led upstairs to be baptized by the ministers. After baptism, I was led into a room for prayer to receive the Holy Spirit. Of course I was already saved, I had just been baptized. But they told me to call on Jesus, he wanted to speak with me today. Jesus wanted to fill all my empty places. So I started saying thank you Jesus, thanking him in advance, because that's what they told me to say. I didn't understand but I did it anyway.

Something strange happened while praying, I felt the Lord's presence. I knew then that I could go further in the Lord. But I couldn't pray anymore. Thoughts started ringing in my head: You mean to tell me there's something more?!

You mean to tell me I am missing something?! You mean to tell me I didn't have everything I needed from the Lord! I couldn't believe there was something more! What was all this living for? All those battles fought, all the victories won, and I'm still undone?! I couldn't go any further, my mouth said thank you Jesus, but my heart was torn from the shock of something more.

A year had passed, then my sister came to me and said, 'It seems like you have gotten worse since you've been baptized. Do you want the Holy Spirit? We can pray right now.' Yes, I replied. Nobody had to tell me his spirit was real, I felt his presence. And this time, I repented, I hadn't done that before. Then I cried out to the Lord, for he knew in my heart what I was searching for: I wanted to go further in the Lord. It didn't matter what I sounded like or what I said, like a newborn baby, I was open. I heard myself speaking in words I didn't understand, but more importantly, I heard the Lord saying, 'Now spread my word.'

AT FIRST

At first you were just a belief taught by others. I couldn't see my need for You. I was coming because of others' expectations

Then you were a show I played in with others. I couldn't see my need for You. I was too busy thinking of my lines.

Then you were a competition. I couldn't see my need for You. Comparing myself to others took too much of my time.

Then you were my Comforter, when I started needing something new. Despite what others expected, You simply told me I was Yours and You were mine.

TO BE REBORN

To be reborn to pass from death to life, to surrender one's all to the Lord, letting the King of Glory come in.

When He makes his presence known, you can feel the warmth He brings. Like a splash of oil upon one's head, you can feel the anointing.

All of a sudden there's an urgency, like holding the door to a river that's ready to flow. Now that He's got you in his arms, don't be afraid to let go. Other tongues will flow as He takes control, and you will know that He is within you.

I did not hear HIS audible voice, nor see a visible hand; but by faith I knew the same God who said 'Let there be', and it was, had spoken, through ME, once again!

MY EDEN EXPERIENCE

There were no mirrors there. I only knew how my Love saw me. Growing up was different there in the garden I had everything at my feet. My Love gave them to me for me to keep.

I fiddled around with things to find out what they would bring me. I tried my hand at building things, but it seemed my hand was too heavy. My Love stepped in and showed me how, He knew just what to do. Thereafter my Love was there to simply guide me through. He would step in and let me know just when my work wouldn't do; He did it by simply showing me an easier way to.

We walked a piece to somewhere new, I met someone there too. That someone wanted chores out of me I didn't feel right doing. My Love saw me and said, that person's taxes are too high for me he would have me doing things I wasn't comfortable (compelled into) doing. My Love took me home and left me alone as He did those chores for me. I watched my Love and much to my surprise the chores I thought I'd never do, I found myself compelled to do so.

That someone new I saw before approached me once again. He said open my eyes, can't I see, there's no love or beauty in me, only in the Love whose hand I was holding. So I gazed down on myself to discover the beast within me. Without my Love I found myself bitter and sarcastic, proud and unthankful, self-centered and envious, greedy and promiscuous, phony and having a false sense of security.

How could my Love, love someone like me? How am I pleasing? So I sought to do things to change me.

I found there was truly a difference between my Love and me, for my self-inflicted wounds didn't even tame me. The peace in the chore of loving and giving was still missing. I grew weary, sweating, trying to change me. But I kept inflicting, sometimes pretending, for fear of disclosing the beast that raged within me. Where is my Love? What happened to me? Where is my Love to inspire me, to compel and empower me?

An offer was made by my Love to transform me into the loving person I long to be. By the Son of my Beloved, I now have his Love growing inside of me.

AN ODE TO MY LOVE, THE EVERLASTING FATHER, MY PRINCE OF PEACE

MY MUSICAL LOVER

My love is a musician who plays on the strings of my heart.

His melodies are soothing.They make you forget everything. His melodies are breathtaking. They make you want to cry.

My love is a composer who chooses the words I sing. The words are encouraging, just singing them brings pleasure.

Tell me, is your love a talented musician, who plays on the strings of your heart?

LOVE ME?

Are your melodies from the bottom of your heart?

Is your love too deep for you to depart?

Is your love too solid to tear apart?

Is your love everlasting, will it endure all things?

Or will you discard me if I cause shame?

Do you really love me from the bottom of your heart?

FOOT WASHING

Having been born again of the water and the Spirit, all things have been made new. The Holy Spirit on the inside gives a fresh new start as he leads and guides. However, every now and then, as you walk this Christian walk, a foot washing is needed. Meaning, you don't need to be born again, again; because you are already fresh, new, cleaned. However, you need a cleansing or correction of thought every now and then. And it takes humility on both ends for the washing to be received. Jesus said in John 13:7 KJV, 'What I do thou knowest not now; but thou shalt know hereafter.' The Lord was teaching them something more. We will ALL need our feet washed from time to time spiritually. Allow me to share with you the testimony of how the revelation of foot washing was revealed.

I was at a weeknight teacher's meeting, requesting prayer for a situation at work. I'd had enough of this coworker deliberately doing things to aggravate me. So I asked the teachers to agree with me in prayer that whatever pit was laid, let the person fall into it. Let his mischief return upon his own head. Don't let his head go down in peace. Being the wordings from my request were taken from King David's writings in scripture, I felt justified in using them.

One of the teachers, who was also a deacon in the church, replied, 'We are going to pray. But you know, we have something David didn't have, we have the Holy Spirit! So Jesus commissioned us to love our enemies and to pray for those who despitefully use us. I'm sure the coworker needs the Holy Spirit. So we are going to pray for the person, not on the person. Is that alright?' My response, without thinking, was 'Wow! You just washed my feet!'

At that very moment the meaning of true foot washing was revealed to me. As you walk this Christian walk, you need your feet washed. I needed to reconcile the old testament with the new testament with a good washing of the word. Deacon delivered the message with the right spirit; he didn't come judgmental, stating how long I've been saved and how I should know better. No, he looked beyond my fault and saw my need. So I was able to receive the message with the same spirit of humility in which it was given. This is true foot washing! ***Every*** child of God will get their feet dirty while walking, and we need foot washers who will look beyond the fault to serve what is needed.

HELP ME TO LOVE

He lied!! Why did he lie? Why the sorry story, was it just to get by? I was getting punished for his lies!! Not only was I getting punished but it was costing me!! This wasn't someone trying to impress; we were only friends. This was just plain deceit, nothing less! Lord, I know it's wrong for me to feel this way; so I'm going to need your help today! Help me to love him because I think I hate him. The most I can do right now is avoid him.

Thank you Lord for allowing me to avoid him. I know it's wrong for me to feel this way, so help me to love, for your namesake. I know this is becoming a song, admitting my feelings are wrong. I need to be strong. For what is service, if it's not pleasing? Why say, I give, without an offering (the best is surrendering oneself)? Every call has a cost. Lord give me strength to carry my cross.

It's been a few months, Lord, but I can now say, you reward those who diligently seek you! Thank you for helping me to love, for your namesake! Your love goes beyond forgiveness to friendship!

FAKE SLEEPING

Who's sleeping? Not me!

I'm hiding in my fantasy. It's so much better than reality!

What?! Who's knocking? I'm sleeping!

How does Mom know when I'm pretending? Didn't know at the time, but God was interceding.

STOP THE PICTURES

Lying in my bed, it happened again. The pictures flashed in my mind like a movie scene.

I could hear the voices like an alarm in my head. I didn't stop it, I just let it go on.

My thoughts took me to a world of my own. It had no regard as to where I went or how long I was gone. I go on pretending like nothing went wrong. But I'm not a remote; I've lost control. The pictures now play like a violin in my soul.

Oh Lord, give me strength to get out of this bed. Stop the pictures from playing, show me the alarm instead.

ADDICTION

In a routine for a simple high cause it keeps the mind occupied
and the head up in the sky.

Emotions are the caves that bring captivity, and hopelessness
is the chain that binds productivity.

Everything visible becomes an enticing invitation, a different
stimulation than one's present situation: nicotine, alcohol,
drugs, work, sex, food and affection.

Every user claims he knows his limitations, but no matter the
measure it becomes an addiction.

Oh, it's easy to say break free, yet everyone is drowning in
their own hopeless sea.

A CHANCE TO BREAK FREE

My shoe came untied and he dropped to his knees. Wow! I'm at work! Can they smell my need? Okay Lord, I see I need to pray. Because, I'm no sleaze, a medal to be worn on someone's sleeve.

Thank you Lord! Now, I see! All this time you were waiting on me. The Lord is giving me a chance to break free. I'll tell the Lord my need; He promised to satisfy, guaranteed! Some things come by prayer and fasting; this will come by prayer, fasting, witnessing and no idling.

RESTORATION

In the beginning you know He's real. It's not just something you think but it's the joy you feel, the anointing in prayer and your spiritual zeal.

As time progresses you falter to the taste of sin. You come to church to get involved, join a committee to take charge. But somehow, you're steeped in the carnality that you're in. At times you look around at others and you feel no condemnation. You wonder now if God exists. Tell me, are you hooked like this?

I found out the cause of my sin. I grew relaxed in the grace God allowed me to be in, and as I relaxed, pride took over. I stopped using prayer to look over my shoulder. I was seeking; yet I wasn't praising God with my living and giving. I was looking at the fruits of God thinking that they were my own: looking at people God meant to draw unto him as my pedal stone. I was allowing myself to be vexed by the enemy showing me the pleasures received from the world, which took away my pleasure of walking by God's Word.

All of a sudden, I grew wise in my own deceit. So God allowed me to live but he removed his hand far from me. Because he could not walk with the proud or the scornful - those who looked low on others. Seeing my carnality in its full view, I grabbed for the hand that was lifted from me. But my flesh was holding me down, so that I couldn't reach out. It was letting me see I was filthy, by accusing me as being unworthy. It was no longer seductive, but condemning.

I cried out to the Lord while fasting, fearing never to reach his hand. I cried out in pain, wanting to be released from the misery my own deceit got me in. I was thinking in my own understanding, preferring a lie instead of praying for understanding.

Totally humbled, I reached my hand out, no longer looking at myself but trying to grab others as I clung to God's hand - his unchanging hand, determined now with prayer to shut myself in.

Now I always try to remember others who are in the same carnality that I was in, and with love, try to draw them in. I try to stay humble so I won't slip back in the fear of the enemy - which is brought on by the pride of men.

Awake O souls that are in the dust. God has said you can now sing. Separate yourselves and be holy as you enter in. Then shut the door and lock yourselves in. The night comes when it will be too dark to see other friends to soothe yourself within.

BURNING SENSATION

This burning sensation that I feel, needs Your Love, Your touch, Your zeal.
I need Your Love to penetrate deep within my soul, to remove my insecurities and make me whole;
I need the assurance of Your Love to keep me both spiritually and physically.
I need to be in Your Loving care, to feel the warmth from You being there.
This burning sensation that I feel, needs your Inspiring Love to heal.
Thank you for a love so powerful, so real!

An Ode to my Love, my Counselor, my Prince of Peace

LOVE'S FULFILLMENT

His lips drip with milk, and like milk it builds up my body!
His kiss dazzles my tongue and heightens my senses.
His words are pure water; it filters out and removes all uncertainty.
His love is hearty; it fills me up and sustains me for days.
His caresses are herbs; it gives me the energy and boost I need.
His love is truly fulfilling.
Whenever I'm with him, I feel a rush. He's my dream; my first real crush!

THE LIGHT OF LOVE

The light of Love warms the heart; it gives hope when times are hard.

Like a sunlit sky, it changes the way one sees.

Like the moon, it keeps darkness from running over like the sea.

Like the stars, its contentment sheds new light on your destiny.

Like the dawn of a new day, the light of love shows you in a better way!

The light of love is God's cavalry.

THE PENETRATING SEASONS OF LOVE

Love digs deep within the heart of an individual and plants seeds in the cold. Love doesn't stop at what it sees; it searches to find one's deepest desire and its roots grab a hold.

Love challenges one to be strong, as it builds integrity. Love digs deep within the heart bringing out one's doubts and insecurities. Anger and fear try to fight love with shame. It piles dirt upon it to cause it pain.

But, the power of love is strong; it can penetrate through anything.

The strength of love is in its reign of expectation. And for every downpour, love will surely spring.

However, love comes with seasons: It appears cold when you learn to let go, stormy while you wait to grow, and sunny when things just flow. Then sooner or later you will know, no matter how things fall, love's beauty will still show.

I DIDN'T KNOW

I didn't know she was abused as a child; I just knew she seemed wild. Then one day it came out in a table discussion. 'With marriage comes honor and the bed is UNDEFILED!' She thought the desires she had made her bad; so she acted out accordingly.

Wow! This wasn't just a friend, it felt like family. I told her, 'No! What that man did to you was wrong; he stole your innocence! Don't you dare let this thief make you feel you don't belong!

God designed marriage to take care of your physical needs; in the bed with your husband, you can do as you please!

Give God all your fears, needs and insecurities. He already gave his best so that you could find rest.

WORK WHILE IT IS DAY

Though it was late, I set out because the Spirit of the Lord was leading me to go and write. The street lights and the highway markings were all I needed for the five hour journey that night. I was driven by the knowledge that God was sending me to get the work done. It didn't seem to faze me that the street lights disappeared and the only thing left was the markings on the highway; I arrived with no trouble because my heart was set on getting to my destination to finish my work. The zeal of the Lord was upon me.

The way back was different. I left early but the darkness seemed to envelop me. I had to drive extra slow to ensure that I could see the road. The markings on the highway seem to fade into nothing. I found myself looking for someone to follow. Then I saw the light from the factories in the distance, though not close to the road, they shined like lanterns during a blackout. I thanked God for their lights shining so that I could see. When I came upon street lights, I praised God even more.

Then I understood the scripture: work while it is day, for when night comes no man can work. While the zeal or light of the Lord is shining on you to do, do it. Because it becomes easy to follow others around you when you lose sight of what the Lord told you. When you don't move when the Lord lays it on your heart to move, it's hard to do it later unless you have others who are letting their light shine.

THE TREE IN ME

Here I sit, just plain soil, without a clue of what I should be. A bunch of different trees surround me. I looked at all the trees; all had different shapes and styles right down to their leaves. And they maintained their beauty even when things were falling apart. Of course, when the weather grew hard, all submitted to the will of God.

In time, one tree in particular put a soft spot in me. I knew right away I wanted to be that tree. So I opened my soil and said, 'please let your seeds fall down on me.' Surprisingly, every tree started dropping seeds; and my soil was opened to everyone. However, only one tree took root inside of me, and I became that tree.

As time progressed, I saw this hard soil looking up at me. What on earth did this soil want? He is not my responsibility! What does life expect from me?! Strangely something happened, I could feel Mother Nature pulling something out. Suddenly seeds sprung out of me, like water falling between my leaves. Then I knew my responsibility, for Mother Nature was letting me see, life could actually come out of me!

GAZING ON MISTAKEN PEACE

I sat gazing in someone else's window. It was not by choice; I had to look by. The walls were thin as if they were glass; and no one could ignore the sorrow within.
A storm hit the people; all anyone could do was pray. Shelter exists inside the walls, but they must hold fast. All will have to weather the storm, but only one must surely last.

I can see tension on her face. She's not at peace, she's worrying. She puffs at a cigarette, sips a drink. The lines on her face seem to fade.
Yet hours later the lines reappear with a permanent indentation of a peace that was mistaken.

THE WATER THAT KILLED MY FLAME

For a year and nine months I was allowed to release my anger on him. They told me he was to blame; he was the one who killed my child. They told me stories to prove their claims. The pain inside of me was like fiery flames. I poured my anger, regret, bitterness and hatred on this man like fire. I threw it all at him. He killed my son! He killed my son! He is to blame!

Nine months they fed me someone to take the blame. Releasing my grief was like soothing medicine. The comfort was having someone to beat. After we get through beating him, then we can bury this matter by totally destroying him.

Then the opposition came declaring his innocence. I don't care about their truths: He was the water that killed my flame! How dare they say he's not to blame! What are they trying to do? I could see if they were taking him because they found someone new. But they plan to take him without a clue. Are you telling me to put that anger and bitterness back on my chest, along with all the unspoken words and regret? No! I will not allow the fire to be rekindled again! For a year and nine months he took the blame. This matter has to die for me to have rest. So I plan to destroy him till there's nothing left!

Inspired by the Not Guilty verdict of murder in the 1st degree.

WHO WAS THAT PERSON?

Who was that person? He acted like an animal. The further I keep him away from me the better. Maybe if I dressed in respectable clothes, he won't come around me. What?! This man is plaguing me!! He may look studious and work in respectable clothes, but he is definitely out of control. How do I get this animal away from me? Looks like all he does is fight to gain control. It's as if others are a threat to him or an invasion of his territory. I'm beginning to believe he takes pleasure in hurting others to get what he needs. He needs to take a good long look in the mirror.

What's this I see? The animal I've been watching is I! What's wrong with me? I think the animal I learned about in history is still living inside of me. I wonder if my mother knew or if anyone else could see. Please could you check to see if an animal is hiding inside of me?

OH LORD I COME

Oh Lord I come to thee, Heavenly father, you are my fortress, keep me safe.

When trials are pressing me, and I don't know what to do, send your arms of protection. Lord, let me hold on to you; only you can see me through

When my faith is shaken, by all the things I see, and it seems your promises, are far from reality, give me courage to stand for thee.

Oh Lord I come to thee, Heavenly father, you are my fortress, keep me safe.

When I'm feeling lonely, and no one understands, give me assurance you'll always be my friend; let me feel your outstretched hand.

When questions come to mind, with answers I can't find, show me your will is a plan of true love divine. Give me peace of mind.

Oh Lord I come to thee, Heavenly father, you are my fortress, keep me safe.

Lord you are my strong tower, all power is in your hand. All things consist, and are here, by your command. Lord give me the strength to stand.

Oh Lord I come to thee, Heavenly father, you are my fortress, keep me safe. Oh lord I come to thee, give me the strength I need. Oh Lord I come to thee

SHADES AND HEALING

Protection
comes in all types of colors,
we often call shades.

HEALING

When peace is given
by the mending of the heart,
they call it healing.

SILENT REFLECTIONS

Silence brings trouble,

its reflection disturbs peace,

but answers bring relief.

A HOME

Homes built with care last,

because the elements are the same.

Build on Jesus' name!

MY MOTHER'S TOMB

My Father came into the bedroom where my sister and I were sleeping. "Get up." He told me. "I have to take your Mother to the hospital." I hopped out of bed, put some clothes on over my pajamas, and woke up my sister lying beside me. I told her what Dad said, and she woke up my brothers. The fact that Mom had to go to the hospital was nothing new; she's been to the hospital several times. I guess I really wasn't worried; I didn't know if my Mother was overreacting or not.

I walked into the hallway where my Mother was standing. When I looked at my Mother standing there not able to speak or breathe properly I knew something was wrong. Still I didn't want to believe it. Everything seemed to be happening quickly without any warning. I helped my Mother get into some clothes. Dad was rushing; at this point Dad decided he could no longer wait on the ambulance. So we all headed outside, but just as we were leaving the ambulance came.

No one could ride in the back of the ambulance, and only one person could ride up front. So my Father rode in the ambulance. My brothers and sister stared at the ambulance crying. I couldn't drive so I had to depend on my brothers and sister to drive. I turned to them crying, "Please pull yourselves together! Somebody has to drive to the hospital. I can't drive."

When we arrived at the hospital they had already wheeled my Mother inside. A nurse came out into the waiting room and asked us to wait in the family waiting room. We all felt Mom was a priority patient, so we didn't think it was strange we were asked to be separated from the others waiting. So we all got up and went inside this small room. The doctor came in and asked, “Can you tell me what happened?” My Father proceeded to tell him, "My Wife and I were up watching a movie together when she had trouble breathing." Afterwards we all joined in the conversation to relay how we ended up at the hospital. Once we finished telling our story we found out the reason for the small separate room. The doctor said, "I'm sorry, she didn't make it." This small private room was not to wait for the living; it was to announce the dead.

> I died today. My spirit failed me and now I am the walking dead. I tried praying by putting my request on the altar and leaving it there; but I don't think He picked it up. If He spoke I didn't hear what He said.

After we calmed down from the Doctors announcement, we were taken to see Mom. As we were being escorted to the hospital room where she laid, I could only think of all the times we’ve been to the hospital, this time we'll be coming home without Mom. When we reached the room, we all walked inside. I looked at my Mother’s face, her tongue was hanging out, twisted, from where they tried to revive her. I couldn’t say a word; I could only stand there and look. I moved in closer to touch her, but she wasn’t there. This wasn’t the same person, she was cold. The person I knew was warm, strong, and full of life. The woman that lie before me had no life in her. Touching her was like touching a brick house. She couldn’t feel my hand; she didn’t acknowledge me reaching out. This wasn’t my Mother; this was an empty tomb. This knowledge gave me strength to say yes to the will of God, for I knew her spirit had been caught up into the heavens, where she'll rest up there in the Promised Land.

To say we don't feel the loss of love because we are Spirit-filled christians is misleading. However, we have peace in knowing our love is in the Father of Love's hands. Loss occurs when what was once there has been removed. Naturally you want to bridge the gap, to replace what was lost. The temptation to reach for things or people we shouldn't is strong. It is at this time you are the most vulnerable and the Lord, the Body of Christ is most needed. From heartaches we learn, what you do to the least of us affects the whole body. A tear left untreated can cause an infection.

CAN YOU MAKE IT?

A weary load on one little heart. Can you make it?

The pound, that pushes the load up and down, for all of it to come down harder the next time around. Can you take it?

Oh, but, you're still going on and on, with weakness inside making it really rough. How long will you fake it?

Your heart begins weakening, with the pounds getting weaker, and all the love that your heart bore comes out in front of you. But by this time, your heart beat is gone . . . And time . . . is standing still. Now the memories and the trials are left for someone else to steal.

The future is carried on like the past.

Can you make it? Can you take it? How long will you fake it?

TO MAKE IT EASIER

I don't know what to say, I don't know what to do. I don't know what to say or do to make it easier. Do you?

The battle seems long, the nights seem gray. But I keep holding on, hoping he will make a way.

I don't know what to say, I don't know what to do. I don't know what to say or do to make it easier. Do you?

I go to work waiting till my day is through, all the while thinking of what I'd rather do.

I don't know what to say, I don't know what to do. I don't know what to say or do to make it easier. Do you?

I'm riding out time while seeking his face. Hoping for abundant life, as he bestows on me grace.

Because I don't know what to say, I don't know what to do. I don't know what to say or do to make it easier. Do you?

I REACH OUT TROUBLED

I've tried and I've failed, now I reach my hand out. Won't anybody take it?

I need help in this world. Won't anybody help me to make it?

I know everybody cries, but I've tried and tried. So now I reach my hand out. Won't anybody take it?

Please help me, please. Just give me a hint or a clue, anything will do. I reach my hand out to you with the life lines that are almost due. Is there anybody in this world with a love that's true?

Would that person of love by any chance be you?

WHEN YOU'RE TROUBLE

When you're troubled and you're hurting, don't know what to do, Jesus says

just come to Me as you are, give your all to Me.

Just come to Me as you are; I'll be your friend.

And through your darkest nights, I'll be your bright and morning star.

LETTING GO TO MEET IN THE AFTERLIFE

How do you say goodbye to love? How do you let it go? How do you say goodbye, to being needed by someone, who needed you? My zeal, my very inspiration is gone. How do you handle this loss? How can one even call this just a loss? It's so much more.

God gives love so we can live. He gives a parent's love to remind us we're special. He gives a spouse' love to let our feelings show. He gives a child's love to remind us we continually grow. God is love, how can I just let love go? No! I'll just keep occupying myself until God gives the next flow.

Everyone is praising the outgoing year; but I'm on my knees with my eyes full of tears. The only thing I can remember is my loss. The passing of my Mother is a heavy cross. What is wrong with me? Why can't I sing? Death still has a sting. You never really know what you've lost until it turns up missing. All the fussing, all the checking, and the activities together, what a blessing!

Thank you Lord for a love so strong. You were the love, you are the song. You were my warmth all along. Thank you for the people you put in my life, to show your love, till we meet in the afterlife.

MOTHERS, FATHERS, HUSBANDS, WIVES AND STEPS

I won't say I understand your pain but I do know grief; I know how it feels to adjust. Since the time I was born, before I could talk, I've always known them as Mom and Dad. Mom was never 'Father's wife' and Dad was never 'Mother's husband,' if so it was before we were born. They were there to take care of us, sacrificing their lives for us; we even vacationed together.

Now Mom is gone and Dad has moved on. We all felt the heaviness of the separation; we all experienced the loss. And in our own way we must all learn how to say, Father's wife, and even, Mother's husband. Strange as it may sound, it's a lesson that must be learned. Fathers are, and can be, husbands, just as well as new husbands can be Fathers. And Mothers are, and can be, wives, just as well as new wives can be Mothers.

STEPS

We are family though we don't share DNA. We were brought together in another kind of way.

Instantly brothers and sisters without any prep, a part of a union, we've learned to call steps.

I KNOW

I know I can be happy! Jesus is risen, He's risen!
I know death thought he had me, but he didn't, he didn't
I know because Jesus sent me back His Spirit, His Spirit
I know I can be happy; Jesus is risen, He's risen
He's risen!
I don't have to feel down because of where I am.
Jesus is risen!
It does not yet appear what I shall be.
Jesus is risen!
He gives power over the chains within
Jesus is risen, He's risen
I know I can be happy; Jesus is risen, He's risen
I know death thought he had me, but he didn't, he didn't
I know because Jesus sent me back His Spirit, His Spirit
I know!!

THE QUEST FOR COMFORT

We are born with a need for warmth, food and cleanliness; however, this need is met by someone else. As we get older, our need for independence causes us to supply our own needs. Yet, it doesn't bring with it the same warmth.

Thus begins the search for comfort, this thing we call love.

The problem is how to receive this love without surrendering one's independence. We don't mind being willingly bound, as long as we are free. We don't want to be held by fear or abuse, as in slavery. We want warmth because of the comfort its presence brings. With the right warmth, we learn sacrificing, though bound, can make you complete.

Believe it or not, there is a Comforter; his name is Jesus. He'll soften your heart with His words, and his kindness will cause you to sing!

THE MALL LIFE

They're all lined up for display, each with his own spirit, his own character.

They stand arrayed waiting to be picked.

They don't mind if you try them; they want to capture you.

They come prepared for every occasion. But if you are looking for one to match your personality, only one is really suitable.

It becomes hard to deny them without really trying them!

IS THIS HOW YOU WANT IT?

'Is this how you want it, like this?! Not like this!' I could hear the Spirit of God whispering in my ear. At the same time, I could hear my friend saying, 'Aren't you curious?'

My body wasn't flamed; I thought I would be raptured. 'You've been saying no for so long. Aren't you curious?' 'Is this how you want it, like this?!' Back and forth, I could hear the battle within me.

I knew when I came to his house, it wasn't to watch a movie. Contrary to Eve, I wasn't deceived. The question is, who would I let use me? Covered in shame, I left that day. I let the Spirit use me. I dressed with haste, my virginity in place; thanking God I wasn't date raped.

THE STATE OF WHO I AM AND IMAGE

Like an embryo still wrapped in a water bag, I was surrounded in a sea of darkness, without purpose, not knowing what or how I should be, without hope, until the Spirit brought light. Like an umbilical cord that provides nutrients to the unborn, the Spirit brought purpose, destiny, love and hope; and when it came, it was like a tree of life. The Spirit's love, power, and peace of mind were the substance that one hopes for. The Spirit was light in the darkness.

Grown, though still a preemie, pushing for independence from the only one I can depend on. Like a water bag breaking, and the baby flowing out, the umbilical cord was broken; the connection between the Spirit (that brought new life) and I severed. The living waters, that once gave light, were withdrawn leaving a sea of darkness, and my true hopeless state came to the surface.

Why is image so important? Why does it matter what others see? Is it that I'm just arrogant? Do I really want followers, a bunch of others just like me?

Perhaps I want customers, but what am I selling? What's this need to be pleasing? Does it have anything to do with the image reflecting back at me?

Inspired by Genesis Chapters 1 and 3

A VESSEL OF LOVE

I wasn't sure whether I wanted Jesus to use me to Love so freely.

Somehow, the Lord involved my heart, so that I had to give. I knew when I started giving that this was how God wanted me to live.

There are many things, from Love, I thought I wouldn't take. But without Love, my Lord, my heart would break.

Sometimes the trials can be tough, but when it comes to Love, it seems you just can't give enough. Now I know why Jesus hung his head and died. Yes Lord, yes, for Love, I'll be crucified.

Thank you, Lord, for your Spirit of Love you gave so freely. Thank you, Lord, for your Spirit of Love and for granting me the liberty!

Lord, I thank you, for swallowing death up in victory, by giving me rest in your arms of Love!

In Loving memory of Gloria

SUBJECTED HEART

The Spirit of Love wrestles against the thoughts in my mind bringing out hidden desires I cannot define. It holds me captive to what's discovered, uncovered.

To whom does one complain? Where does one go?

The Spirit of Love has tamed me, wherever it leads me, I go. I hope the love it used to capture me, will one day, soon release me.

Tell me, would the Spirit of Love bind up the heart, without setting it free?

CONSIDER LOVE

Consider love, while thinking of life and death. Love produces life, love makes life worth living. Death separates, it shatters dreams and destroys expectations. Yet, even still, love can bring the dead spirit back to life again.

THE SECRET PLACE

Lord, you are the author of the supernatural, the scientifically unexplainable! Thank you for satisfying and keeping me in your secret place! The more I depend on your miraculous hand, the more I feel its need to stand. Allow me to share this truth: there is a secret place in Christ, where your need is met in such a way, it gives you exceeding joy without fault! I am a kept woman because of this secret place! Whether in the body or out of the body I don't know, but it gives new meaning to Jude 1:24-25.

Okay Lord, why can't your will be done on Earth as it is in heaven? Don't be mad at me, but why can't the spiritual meet the natural already? And please don't silence my complaints by taking away this secret place. I know it's a walk by faith and not by sight; but one of the hardest things to do is to ignore time and wait on You. Besides, what more does he need to receive from You?

Lord! I wanted to find another pair of my favorite leather gloves to replace the one I lost, not a lesson! If I had known this was going to be a lesson and not a recovery, I'd have stayed at home! After three stores, the Lord showed women's gloves were found near the watches. The rest of the outdoor clothing for women were found in another place. Whereas, men's gloves were found with the rest of the outdoor clothing.

Here lies the lesson: Women are willing to step out, but their timing is off because they don't have all they need.

However, men will want all they need before they step out. Thanks.

The secret place is where the Lord uses love to work on the heart. You are miraculously kept; but your heart is exposed to be softened. Emotionally you feel like you are in deep water; but naturally you aren't touched, as if in a see-through submarine. And you wonder, how can this be? The Lord knits the heart, but he protects the body, to work in compassion, understanding, kindness, gentleness, and patience. Now though we have different experiences, we can speak the same language because the feelings are common. The majority of my writings are from the joy and labor pains of this secret place. The expression 'labor pains' is used because I write while waiting for delivery!

P.S. When you start doubting the secret place, you stop dwelling in the secret place and you are no longer under the cover or protection of the secret place.

YOUR LOVE

Your love is like a dream world.

It floats in the air like dust above. Everyone can't see the effect of your love.

Your love found me in the chambers of my mind and grabbed me out of my nightmare. Then you led me to another chamber and told me I could rest there. It was there you sang to me pleasant dreams and sweet realities. I could feel your love rocking me, slowly setting me free. In your love is the key to all my fantasies.

Your love is sweet to me, without it I'm incomplete. Your love is a dream world unfolding into my reality. I never heard a melody, until I met you. I never had a song in my dreams, until I argued with you. Your love makes me sing. Your love is everything! Let me stay before your love.

THE MASK OF PRIDE

The guide who walked along the side of me had on a robe and a staff in his hand. He proceeded to show me a scene with a man whom I knew by the Holy Spirit to be the first earth man, Adam, from the book of Genesis in the Bible. Adam had blood in him; he was connected to a true life source.

But Adam laid down and drained himself of the blood and hooked himself up to a machine that had fake blood. Once he filled himself up with the fake blood, he paraded around like he was somebody important. He would walk around puffed up, with his head in the air. But he wasn't being for real or honest, because the blood wasn't real, it was fake blood. Once the fake blood effect wore off, he would hook himself up again and again.

So I asked the guide that was showing me this 'If it wasn't real, why did he keep doing it?' He responded 'Because by this time it was too late.'

I believe Adam lacked patience with the seasons of life, the time needed for God to make changes in behavior. So the fake blood was a temporary high to mask insecurities, our pitiful mask of pride.

THE BEAST IN THE SEA DREAM

Two people, a male and a female, had to take a journey through the seas. The male's journey was different from the female's journey. The female was in a submarine type vehicle as she traveled and someone was traveling with her. Inside you could see her going through mood changes and speaking in anger. The male was in a suit that covered his body and a beast trailed after him. The male was trying to kill the beast, or get rid of him, with a sword. He would turn around and throw a sword at the beast but the beast kept coming after him. This happened repeatedly, until the beast caught one of the swords with his hand, and began to stab himself with it, to show the man that the sword had no effect on him! In the waters you could see the blood, but it had no effect on the beast, he was still alive! The man stopped swimming and stared in awe at the beast who stabbed himself. Surprisingly, the blood in the water was the blood of the man; it was then that I realized, the man and the beast were one. Suddenly a helicopter came from above, having a great light and a large sword. The sword of the helicopter chopped the head off the beast and the waters abated.

Then Revelations chapter 13 was revealed to me about the beast out of the sea, whose deadly wounds were healed. The sword, the man was throwing at the beast, were attempts at morally good deeds from the bible, that obviously didn't work. Then I understood why the people marveled at the beast in Revelations; they could see no way of conquering the beast; they could see no way of changing. I could see why the beast opened his mouth in blasphemy against God, even the bible could not contain the beast inside. The beast is the selfish uncaring part of us we try repeatedly to beautify or hide, but can't. It is our thoughts, and it leaves its mark on the outside. So, we conclude, there is no conquering the beast and anyone who claims otherwise would be a lie.

But looking deeper into my dreams, I see another side. The battle was not for us to fight, but for the Spirit from on high. And it doesn't matter what version of Word you use, without the Spirit it's not a weapon. The difference between the Word and Sword is the S for the Spirit.

When we receive the same Spirit Jesus had on the inside, he helps to make the Word come alive! Though we can't see Him, He left His Spirit as his mark. This Holy Spirit comes to live on the inside, tackling the beastly thoughts that have us trapped, so that in time, we can shine on the outside. The question is which mark or image will you take – the mark of the LORD or the mark of the beast?

I NEED YOU

Please Daddy; I need you to help me. Keep those thoughts out of my head! I need you to free me. I don't want to be hurt. Please just hide me.

I knew something would go wrong. It was something I did, right? Please forgive me and just keep me. I'll tell everybody it's okay; but Lord I need your help. I bow before you, Daddy, help me.

You are my strength when I am feeling weak. You are my peace when I focus on you. You are the satisfaction that I seek. When my mind tells me otherwise, draw me back in, don't let distraction cause me to sin.

You are merciful; don't let anyone or anything touch me till I hear from you. I need to hear your voice, not thoughts in my head. I feel my body moving, but my heart feels dead. Please Jesus, protect me. Now the LORD knows I need Him; I confessed.

DRIFTING

Drifting like a sheet of paper, love's wind is tossing me to and fro. I'm curious about where it will lead me, but in my heart I'm afraid to go.

At times it gushes and tears me, but it lifts me very high. I feel as if I'm soaring just to kiss the sky!

Then while drifting, out pours my heart's worst fear.

Love shattered me, as if hit by a moving car. No longer drifting, now just flowing, I see the car wheels coming. The end is near.

Falling in his palms, he has caught me. My heart is now all tears.

DESPERATION

Lonely and unattractive is how I feel. Until I met you, I never knew so many emotions to be real.

At first I felt really friendly; I was eager to know and hear more. Then I experienced a hunger, an aching need, to actually taste and feel the sweetness behind the character, which for some reason I grew to adore.

Hot, desperate and desirable, that's how I felt, all my deepest fantasies and desires were tangible. Then I felt cold as if someone removed my cloak.

I'm overwhelmed by you and I've not attempted to hide. Yet, I'm afraid of getting hurt. I don't know where you stand or how you feel.

In the midst of my fantasies are sleepless nights due to my fears and insecurities. I'm weak when it comes to you. I adore how stern you are, yet I'm afraid of being ripped apart. I admire your directness; yet I'm not sure of what's in your heart. I'm fascinated by your confidence; yet I don't know where you stand. Right now, I'm all mixed up inside.

At times, it probably seems like I'm not being real, yet every word that I've written to you is how I truly feel. Tell me, what would a person look for me to do, for proof that my words are true?

ARE WE EVEN FRIENDS? AND THE EMPTY ROOM

I thought we would be friends, maybe best, but when I stop talking, he doesn't speak. The only thing heard is the fear in my head speaking. How can we even be friends?

I'm confronted with his need, but what about mine? Yes Lord, his need and mine entwine, but I fear the other will be lost in time? Without communication, I fear this will end.

Heck, I don't know. Are we even friends?

THE EMPTY ROOM

I open the door to the usual sound. The hum is steady like the sound of a train on tracks. It's blowing out air like a train blows out steam. The atmosphere it makes is cozy.

The surrounding scenery is lovely. The place is furnished and conditioned with air, but no commuter has traveled there.

A FATHER TO COMFORT ME

I feel rejected and alone. I wanted to be a wife; instead, I feel like a concubine without a home. I felt cheap and weak, every time I offered myself, knowing he chose someone else.

He didn't break any promises, because he never made any promises. I feel like letting go, instead, I hide within myself, pretending it didn't matter, but it did.

There's only one escape I've found, I work in the ministry I love, and it keeps me sound. In this I've learned, the joy of the Lord truly is my strength, for I feel loved, wanted, like I belong.

I thank God for the feelings given to me. I thank him for the escape, he's allowed me to see. I'm sharing so that others will see, being a Christian doesn't exempt you, but it gives you a Father who has promised to comfort you.

FLYING FREE

I am free to reach the sky. I am free, like stars on high.

I am free. He said goodbye to me; I am free.

But what is the sky without the sunlight? What are the stars without the moonlight? How can a bird without its wings, how can it ever fly free?

I'm flying, I'm flying, but I can't ever be free. I'm flying, I'm flying but I can't ever be free.

For you are the sun in my sunlight. You are the moon that makes my stars bright. You are the one who gives me wings; you bring the heavens to me.

I am free, my nights are mine. I am free to let dreams unwind.

I am free. He gave up his time with me; I am free.

But what are the nights without company? What is a dream without its fantasy? How can a bird without its wings, how can it ever be free?

I'm flying, I'm flying, but I can't ever be free. I'm flying, I'm flying but I can't ever be free.

For you are the words in my melody. You are the dream in my fantasy. You are the one that gives me wings; you bring the heavens to me.

I'm flying, I'm flying, I'm flying, yeah, yeah, yeah, yeah, baby.

I'm flying, I'm flying, but I can't ever be free. I'm flying, I'm flying but I can't ever be free.

I feel like a bird without its wings. How can I ever be free?

LOVE'S SWING: MY MIND IS MADE UP

I've got my mind made up, I'm never going back again; my mind is made up. I once was blind, but now I see, he's not the only one for me. I've got my own mind made up, made up, made up.

I was following him here and there but I was getting nowhere, wrapped around his thumb trying to persuade that I'm the one.

I once was blind, but now I see, he's not the only one for me, I've got my own mind made up, made up.

I've got my mind made up, I'm never going back again; my mind is made up. I once was blind, but now I see, he's not the only one for me. I've got my own mind made up, made up, made up.

Feeling sorry for myself, I couldn't hear anybody else. My body ached for his affection, but all I got was his rejection.

I once was blind, but now I see, he's not the only one for me, I've got my own mind made up, made up.

I've got my mind made up, I'm never going back again; my mind is made up. I once was blind, but now I see, he's not the only one for me. I've got my own mind made up, made up, made up

It didn't matter when he was mean, I had his voice on the answering machine. Didn't know how bad I looked, now I know that I was hooked.

I once was blind, but now I see, he's not the only one for me,

I've got my own mind made up, made up.

I've got my mind made up, I'm never going back again; my mind is made up. I once was blind, but now I see, he's not the only one for me.

STRANGE HOW YOU SEE

It's strange how you see, no one else wrong but me.

Did you ever holler? Have you ever used strong words? Did you ever wish you were gone, packed your bags and moved on?

It's strange how you see, no one else wrong but me.

Did you ever tell a lie, to keep your secrets inside? Did you ever fill up your time, to keep certain thoughts off your mind?

It's strange how you see, no one else wrong but me.

Did you ever feel you were bound? Did you ever need space to move around? Did you ever wish you could hide from the weakness inside?

It's strange how you see, no one else wrong but me.

THE STRENGTH OF HIS COMING

Three weeks ago I met someone a brother at the State Council. We exchanged names and places of worship, but no numbers; I didn't think much of it because my church is big. And I teach Sunday School, every Sunday morning, and Children's Church on certain Sundays, in a classroom. One and a half week later, I had a dream of someone coming to visit my place who had my name on a piece of paper. In the dream, my neighbors were Caucasians, I had my hair done, and a roommate was staying with me.

Then one week after that, on a Sunday morning I had a dream of just words, "He's coming. Don't let him in." The words were spoken so forcefully, I hopped out of the bed thinking someone was in the hallway of my apartment. A member from the church was spending the night with me, and she hopped up when I ran to the door. I said, 'It's okay. I thought I heard someone in the hallway. It was probably a dream just to wake us up for church. I need time to take my hair down.' (I just had it done yesterday.) It was not too long after I arrived in class, he came.

I didn't connect the dream until the usher led us to our seats. We were seated in front of class visiting from Paris. After the Pastor had them to stand, it struck me, he was the one from my dream. (The roommate for the weekend, my hair being done, the neighbors and him.) Still I rationalized. He's Spirit-filled, has a good job, and his Mom is active in the church. So we continued to converse, after all he took the time to find my class and where it was located to visit. And years had passed since the Lord subjected my heart.

So we would meet for services and chit chat by phone until one Sunday he went to his church. Later, he was so excited about the sermon his Pastor taught; he shared it with me saying, 'When the Lord gives you a warning, listen to it.' I don't particularly like when a man talks about what the Pastor said. I like to hear what

God gave you. Casper and my Father are good examples of sons of God. They shared how God spoke to them through dreams, visions, prayer, and the Word. Remember, God said He would pour out His Spirit on ALL flesh. You don't have to be a Pastor, or have a title. Daughters of Eve, require more from your man, especially since he's born again. Start asking, "What did God deal with you about today? Was it a Word in it for me?" Needless to say, The Lord gave him a Word for me that day; and I knew what I must do. This poem was inspired by our exchange.

He came; I can't believe how strong he came. He made me feel desirable, like a precious gift. I couldn't believe his strength, and he poured all his energy out on me. I felt chosen, set apart. I wondered 'There must be some other motive in his heart.' And God said, "No! Don't let him in."

No other man pursued me like this, his persistence will truly be missed. Yes, he came strong, focused and determined. The strength of his coming sent me on an emotional high. But I knew, from God, the emotional high was not the kind to last forever. And although I enjoyed him coming on to me, God had not yet released me.

Even still, my heart will forever hold the strength of his coming.

Lord, I'm thankful you are here, letting me know you care. Thank you for being patient with my impatience.

SHATTERED EXPECTATIONS

I boast of the Lord, everyone knows he is whom I put my trust. I threaten, and I fuss; but I wait, because I don't want to fight. I want the Lord to fight my battles.

Then the enemy came and with torment he rent my heart; I felt raped, used, exposed, and ashamed.

I can't see the future; I only know what I experienced . . . shattered expectations. God, I hope, will feel my pain when I testify all of this in Jesus' name.

SHADOW OF EMPTINESS

I thought he would take note of me standing there, but he didn't. Reaching out to speak would make me appear desperate, weak, and unstable. After much counseling, I'm supposed to be free of that urgency. I don't want to keep looking back into the cold reality that should have set me free.

So instead of reaching out to grasp the things I thought used to be, I responded to the emptiness offered to me. Slowly I walked away hoping no one could see, the shattered expectations in my eyes and the hurt that still plagues me.

THE ROCK OF LOVE

Forgive me Lord. I know your fires change hearts, continue to soften mine. I put my trust in you for you are love. Yes, you are a rock, but that is why you are a fortress.

The LORD is the rock of love. In His presence there is warmth and provisions, from his reign all blessings flow. He is my covering, my house of protection from storms.

Thank you Father for the love you gave to teach me. Thank you for involving my heart, not my body. Thank you for not leaving me in the hands of man; but entrusting me with a son of God like Isaiah 53.

MAKE US COMPLETE

The Lord's name will be praised. His blessings are so we can't complain.

He designed this garden for us to survive with food, clothing, shelter, and jobs to thrive. Still something is missing, perhaps a zeal and anointing.

Lord lift us high and make us complete before our day is done and we take our seats. According to your mercy, give us the love we need. We realize life is more than our pride and greed.

CAN YOU FOLLOW THE THOUGHT?

A choice on the road, an irresistible gift full of many surprises: new experiences, fresh zeal, and inspired talents are just a few.

Then unexpected ditches: got caught up, occupied with inspired talents, occupation, money and greed.

A lost focus led to negligence, and now a dead end. Have to get back to the gift of inspiration, nothing is greater than the one who inspires.

It was love that inspired me, and love is the precious gift that always delivers!

WHAT ARE YOU IN FOR?

Thank you Lord for asking, 'What are you in for?'

Thank you Lord for revealing your gift is not for my seduction. And the positive response of others is not my lover.

Your gift is just a means to get the message out. You are the true love! You are what life is all about!

TIME

Time is our gift in this brown, blue, and green earth ball that spins. We grasp hold with memories because we know it will end.

Each moment is a flashcard of letters and sounds we define as verbs, adjectives, and nouns. We capture pictures to keep it around, to make what is lost forever be found. Our family and friends and all that are near take part in the celebration of this gift so dear.

A mother tries to make a memory last with the child she holds in her grasp. But surely as the child grows, the little one will loosen his hold. The only thing time will allow are the pictures she holds in the cloud.

Numbers define our progress, until we take our rest. We don't want time to slip away, but we learn of its passing each day. The hourglass hangs like a star in the sky, as a constant reminder we all must die. One time will end, as sure as the earth spins; and a new life will begin.

WHERE IS HOPE?

"Please let me out. Please let me go."

No, life is still going on over here. Come back!

"I mustn't stay. Who is there for me to look back on? Where can I go to where I don't have to turn around and run? Where in this life can you have some fun, without trouble ahead then wishing you hadn't begun?"

You can't go! Hold on to your hopes.

"What is hope, when the things come true, yet only those things that are impossible for you? I must go. I can't hold on any longer. My strength is getting weaker, not stronger. I've got to go. I'm going, I'm sorry but I've got to go. I'm leaving you, I pray to God you make it through. I'll be seeing you, save your last hopes for me. I'll be back, you'll see. Now don't cry!"

Please, no, please. I don't want you to die!

DO YOU STILL DREAM?

At home no one can see I live a dream, apart from reality. I cover my face at times from shame so reality won't see my dream.

At home I dream of true love, in it I willingly give and receive the same. I cover my face at times from shame so reality won't see my dream

At home my hopes are just dreams they don't have to come true. I cover my face at times from shame so reality won't see my dream.

At home sometimes I cry, the truth I can't deny, my dreams are just a dream. I cover my face at times and cry.

I haven't been cured and I know why, because I still dream. Is it a dream or is it hope? Am I smoking weed without the dope? Tell me why can't I cope? Tell me, do you still dream? Lord, you are my head. I'm tired of the dreams, give me a vision instead.

COME BACK

Come back! The Father's telling me. Come back! The Father's telling me, he loves me.

Without the rain., the Father's telling me. Without the sun., the Father's telling me. Without the moon., the Father's telling me, he loves me!

If I shut up Heaven, that there be no more rain, the peace I give this world can't obtain. Then you will hear me.

Come back! The Father's telling me. Come back! The Father's telling me, he loves me.

If my people who are called by my name, would humble themselves and seek my face, then will I heal them.

Come back! The Father's telling me. Come back! The Father's telling me, he loves me.

Without the rain., the Father's telling me. Without the sun., the Father's telling me. Without the moon., the Father's telling me, he loves me!

You labor hard but you get no increase. Satisfaction seems out of your reach. Can't you hear Him calling?

Come back! The Father's telling me. Come back! The Father's telling me, he loves me.

Come unto me, and I'll give you rest. Lay your burdens down off your chest. Hear Him calling.

Come back! The Father's telling me. Come back! The Father's telling me, he loves me.

Without the rain., the Father's telling me. Without the sun., the Father's telling me. Without the moon., the Father's

telling me, he loves me!
Come back!!

A WOMAN WITH AN ISSUE

A crowd was there to meet him before he stepped out. How would I get near him? I was taking a chance being here. If I make a scene people will see me. Everybody has issues, but mine has been declared unhealthy. If they discover who I am, they will call me a mess. I have no other choice but to blend in with the press. I saw someone else get his attention; I heard him accept their invitation. Still if I could just touch him, everything would change. I know in my heart I wouldn't be the same.

Then I touched him! And although I was behind him, it was as if he grabbed my hand. Is this real? What is happening? I feel a miracle happening inside of me! Wait!! He stopped! He's turning around! His eyes searched when he asked, 'Who touched me?' Then his eyes caught mine, trembling. I replied, 'I touched you.' The warmth in his eyes encouraged me, giving me strength to stand. Then he said, 'Your belief in my power to change, has made you complete again.'

Inspired by Matthew 9:19-22, Mark 5:24-34, and Luke 8:42-48

I HAD ALREADY JUDGED

From a distance he looked like a threat to society. I had already judged that he was the kind of person that would bring down my property.

This man was definitely not like me. He wouldn't fit in with the crowd. His manner of conversation would bring him down. He would not be acceptable in our town.

I can imagine how he is at his job. He probably doesn't even know what it means to work hard.

Sometimes life puts us in circumstances where two paths must meet and it would seem inhuman not to speak. Speaking, I found that I was wrong. The man is different, but he's 'human', so I guess he belongs.

FATHER OPEN MY EYES

Father, open my eyes so that I can see. So I can see the things you set out for me, with understanding of what life ahead is going to be. Open mine eyes in the darkness; make a path so I can see the glistening star which leads to all others.

Father, open my eyes so I can see, but without blurriness that can set me apart from thee. Open my eyes to the acknowledgment of the way. Show me the real difference between night and day. Like the sun that shines, let me see the light so that I won't be left behind in the darkness that can blind me. Like the moon, a light where there is none, when darkness is a gate of hate, open my eyes Father, so that I can see.

THE SEED OF EXPECTATION

"I challenge you to surrender the alternatives back. I will not only be your intercessor, but your inter-fess-or. Inter means to bury, to put away, to deposit in the earth. Fess means to tell or make known something that is hidden, doubtful, or to uncover what was buried, deposited and sowed."

I love the vision given me.

You see, God has allowed me to see my petition, and I need it all!

I have the seed of expectation growing inside of me! Sometimes I feel that it is wrong, I shouldn't expect so much. Yet the longer I wait, the more the seed grows.

Is the seed real? Does it have a dad? Did I misinterpret what was said?

God, I hope it was you who showed me my petition. If not, will you be a Father to the fatherless?

LET THE DEAD BURY THE DEAD

This dead state is to refresh my mind of the truth. Reality destroyed my hopes. Every shattered dream serves as an anchor to keep me from drifting off somewhere into a terrible wreck.

Hmm, something strange is happening. Reality didn't shatter my dreams right away. Should I stay in the position that I'm in? Life opened up its doors of opportunity. Should I raise my anchor and let the winds of opportunity cause my dreams to sail free?

Believe it or not, I'm afraid. Should I reach for the same dreams? Maybe I should try obtaining them some other way. Oh my God, what are you trying to say? My dreams just awoke from their dead state today!

I shared my dreams with my friends. Needless to say they didn't understand. They could only remember my despair; I didn't linger with them there. A new fire is burning within me. Let the dead bury the dead, but I'm going to live again!!

BLOSSOMS

Like seasons, trials and expectations, put me through changes. At times I feel betrayed, but I can't afford to be weak. At times I feel spoiled, but I can't afford to be sheltered.

You see, God made me like a flower; I have its blossoms. When it rains, I sometimes grow stronger. But when it really pours, I bend and can't stand up any longer.

The sun shines through the wind, like the birds fly through the sky. It shines on me and my cheeks sprout as I blush. Yet too much sunshine without any rain makes me rot. With strong winds and the sun streaming hot, that flow of water helps out a lot.

Yes, even the wind will betray me, the friend I need to get a breeze. It pushes on me, causing my roots unease. While the dirt kicks upon my face, I try to stand still to keep my petal brain in one place.

When all this comes around, the rain, the sun, the wind, then there's the snow, when things come down heavy. No sunshine, no rain in sight, no strength to back me up in my fight. My mind grows weak and tells me I can't take the pain. But in the clouds, I see the sun as I go down, and I know, deep down in my roots, I'll come back again!

THE TIME AND THE SEASONS

You may be a flower to display beauty for the world to see.
You may be a tree, whose fruits you have to offer are very important to me.
You may be a plant, whose leaves supply us with what we need.
You may be the grass, whose endurance shows us, despite the storms, beauty can last.
Whatever your plight in life maybe, we all have one thing in common:
we have our times, with seasons that pass.

Remember this: It may seem as quickly as it starts, the blossoming beauty is fading away. But in the midst of leaves falling, seeds are falling with hopes of extending life another day.

DON'T SETTLE

I attended a wedding of someone from the job with another coworker who was a Christian. There was a greeter at the door who had an aura about him that reminded me of Casper; plus he was tall, dark and handsome. Once we were seated at our assigned table, the coworker I came with pointed to the greeter and said, 'I could see you with someone like him.' A gentleman at the table was talking to me, then he stepped away for a second. That's when the greeter approached me and asked, 'Are you with him?' No, I replied. 'May I have this dance?' I'm saving my dances for my husband. 'Oh, are you married?' No. 'Then how do you know I'm not your husband?' Thus began a long conversation, which ended in an exchange of phone numbers. For the first time I didn't share who I am, meaning my faith, this young man's aura had me captivated. I felt guilty. A few days later, the question of faith came up. He said, "I believe in God, but I'm not a church goer." But can a person believe someone died or killed for you and yet not want to get together to talk about him or want to meet the person, or know more about the person? No, we do more than that for ball players and people we know on the news. But still, I dropped the ball; I let the comment pass.

That night I had a dream I was Potiphar's wife. Potiphar had me on a pedal stool. Like I could do no wrong. I was thanking God in the dream for not chastising me. Truth be told, despite the aura, I wouldn't just want a son of man when I could have a son of God. So once again, I yielded to God's unchanging hand. Lessons learned: 1) God is large and in charge! He owns the auras! You never have to settle with God., 2) to denying your faith, denies God and who you are., 3) Women were created to help sons of God be all they can be; however you must be born again to follow God's lead., and 4) God has not released me.

ABORTION – HYSTERECTOMY – BARREN

Abortion – Hysterectomy, all my unborn children were snatched away from me

Abortion – Hysterectomy, I can only imagine the faces I will never see

Abortion – Hysterectomy, God, how could this happen to me?

Abortion – Hysterectomy, no birthdays or presents under the tree

Abortion – Hysterectomy, No seeing things for the first time anew

Abortion – Hysterectomy, no dreams or wishes to help come true

Abortion – Hysterectomy, My God, my God what did I do?

Abortion – Hysterectomy – now add Virgin bride, that's me.

Barren – Set aside, grieving what will never be.

Time is now behind me and so is the child I will never see.

STRUGGLING WITH THE ISSUE OF TIME

Struggling with the issue of time and the things I can't see.
Looking for a confirmation or sign for the faith I hold onto daily.
Wondering if I'm losing my mind in a walk that feels like slavery.
Dragging my feet up as I climb each step reveals a new captivity.
Feeling like I'm left behind, all my enemies seem to pass by me.
Naturally I'm no longer blind to my spiritual deficiency.
And yes, I still trust the Father of time, the God who loves me.

THE THINGS YOU CAN'T SEE

I don't want you to face all the challenges that you do; certain things I want to spare you. Certain things you'll expect, others you'll need. But, don't think the things you expect from me are viewed any less than what you need. The fact that you're expecting, shows your trust and confidence in me. And I want you to know how much you are loved. It's not enough for you to be satisfied; you should be pleased.

It won't always be easy following me; some things you won't be allowed to see. The things you can't see may cause you to doubt, without full understanding one can feel left out. But the things you can't see, are the challenges I'm sparing you. Don't doubt my love, for my love is true. I wouldn't withhold anything good from you.

SCHOOL BUS

'Slow down! When you see the school bus, slow down!' I didn't know what the words in the dream meant. Perhaps, children run out in front of cars, so use caution when you drive.

I didn't know what the words in the dream meant until my niece wanted to learn. When I prayed to God, He gave me answers, and I knew this was a gift. It was a pleasure to see growth, to see discovery in someone else's eyes. It restored my youth and gave me a child to cherish. God gave me a gift, and in doing so, He gave me children!

Every member of the Body of Christ is fitly joined to compliment the other.

A GIFT OF VALUE

Is it any wonder I'm weak? I'm a piece of clay being fashioned on a wheel spun by circumstances and events. Is it any wonder I feel spent?

Thank God I have a Father who values me as a pearl of great price. As long as I'm a work of his hands, I trust him with my life. He doesn't want me tarnished and broken causing me to lose value; but he wants me whole. All he asks is I return his love by valuing myself as he does my soul.

I see now with each moment, I am being made anew: a gift of value, a pearl of great price. This is the key to my brand new life. True love is transforming, as long as I value myself as the Father does, I will be showing true love.

LIKE A VIRGIN

Do you feel your lack of knowledge will show? Do you fear you'll get excited too quickly and move or go the wrong way? Wondering whether or not you're desiring something He's willing to give? Is it any wonder that God is the author of Love? I feel like a virgin submitting to His control.

Sometimes I forget his sovereignty and see Him as a man; then I wonder if He knows how to please me. I wonder if my desires please Him, then I'm reminded of how my desires came to be. I didn't know what I desired or what it took to please me, until I met Him. And when He pleased me, I sang His praises and prayed for more. Then He reminded me it's the two of us, not just me.

I hope I don't offend God by looking at others around me. Deception is looking at a hot movie, thinking the responses they show are real. God knows I should not trust the things I see. So, I pray, I will follow Him, and let Him take the wheel. He knows my desires, and He knows just how I feel!!

IMPERFECT DECISIONS

A mistake can cause a set back and fear of rejection.

Disobedience can cause separation with loneliness as its weapon.

Imperfection can cause abandonment and questioning of choices. Are things out of sorts because of something I did or did not do?

Maybe my desires could be wrong and I'm being punished till they change. The truth is I fear the whole situation: the rejection, separation, abandonment, and having to face choices.

THE VALLEY OF DECISION

Lord, we long to be free, yet at times it feels like we're not meant to be. Maybe our fears have us down. We feel trapped by images surrounding us. The outcome of others leads one to believe that hope is just a dream. Some outcomes are disastrous, which causes one to fear his own. Others are blessed so quickly; it makes one wonder what he is doing wrong.

Lord, you see the dilemma this world is in? We feel bound by fear: each decision carries the punishment of its sin. To some this may not seem major, a decision only takes a second to make, but a decision can cost you a lifetime for one little mistake.

KINGDOM LESSONS

Entering the kingdom, it's understood, you are under the rules of another. As a citizen of the kingdom, you are free to go in and out. Leaving one place to visit another, your mind has a tendency to wonder.

If you're on the inside, but your mind is still outside, wondering if you should pursue, this is what God will do: He'll take those thoughts one by one and show you his way is true.

You may experience pain as he breaks your thought chains. But a good teacher uses problems as a test, to check your answer and to teach what is best.

So whether you stayed in or stepped out, rest assured God will correct you without a doubt.

ENVY AND JEALOUSY

Like open wounds, jealousy and envy still plagues me. I wonder if I were where I wanted to be in life, would they still bother me.

Was there a lesson I didn't learn? The fire is gone, yet I still feel the burn.

I wonder if someone else can see, jealousy is holding my promise, and envy is where I should be. My fear is I have to wait until I'm all I should be before my desire is given to me. This fear disables me, despite the need, despite the urgency.

Maybe when faith overcomes my fears, envy and jealousy will be a defeated enemy.

UNTIL I'M DESTINED

I've been running around the streets of this town, looking for peace, that's out of my reach. I feel like I'm searching.

I can pay all my bills, but there has to be more. I'm looking for satisfaction that isn't a chore. I feel like I'm searching.

But until I'm destined to go somewhere, I might as well sit back and relax. Yes, until I'm destined to go somewhere I might as well sit back and relax.

I look to my friends to help me unwind; but nobody's there to ease my mind. I feel like I'm searching.

I look all around at what I can see, but nothing really captivates me. I feel like I'm searching.

But until I'm destined to go somewhere, I might as well sit back and relax. Yes, until I'm destined to go somewhere, I might as well sit back and relax.

I cry out to the Lord for he knows what's in store. He knows in my heart what I'm looking for. I'm tired of searching.

So, until I'm destined to go somewhere, I might as well sit back and relax. Yes, until I'm destined to go somewhere, I might as well sit back and relax

THANK YOU LORD FOR WHO I AM

Lord, I thank you for making me.

Thank you Lord for continually changing me; yes, even the changes I've yet to see.

Thank you Lord for helping through the pain I bear. Thank you Lord for listening and letting me know you care.

Thank you Lord for the Love you give; love is what I need and want to live.

Forgive me Lord for always wanting more, and not waiting for whatever you have in store.

Forgive me Lord for fearing what is to come, when I should just trust that your will be done.

I GET JOY

When I think about what I should be and what I know I am, I get weary and discouraged, I give in within. But the Lord comes and delivers me. It's a comfort to know he still cares. He knew I wouldn't be satisfied, til he changed me on the inside.

I get joy from my pain in life. Oh, I get joy, I get joy.

I know when I stumble and fall, from the shame and hurt, he changes my ways. The person I thought I could never be, by his grace and mercy, he shows me I can.

Now if you doubt you could be free, Jesus will show you that you can.

And you'll get joy, you'll get joy. Oh you'll get joy, you'll get joy.

AFRAID TO BE FREE

Life is an array of painted pictures on display. It takes courage to display the sketches my way.

Still, I lay out my plans for what I picture life will be. No one knows how it will turn out but I paint on expectantly.

Mentally I'm struggling to keep a certain view, without it being distorted by others with pictures too.

Sometimes people throw splotches of paint on my drawing, because they don't like what they see. It hasn't been labeled acceptable; therefore, it just can't be.

So I wait until my picture is clear so I can see what I used to see. Sometimes, while I'm waiting, I feel bound with pressure; and I become afraid.

Do I really want people to see my sketch of life with all the mistakes I've made?

Maybe I should rethink my task. Do I really want to expose my feelings, or would I prefer to paint a mask? Maybe I should stop and listen to others and what they say I should have?

So I stop and I listen, and I paint life's pictures, not for myself, but for others and what they say it should be. I follow the sketch of someone who is acceptable, and probably afraid to be free.

JESUS, I CAN CALL ON YOU

When there's nowhere else to run, no one else to tell my problems to, I can always count on you. I know that you allow pain for a reason, even if it appears to last longer than a season.

You love me! I know this to be true. You know me! I don't have to hide from you. You include me! I was a part of your plans from the beginning.

Tell me, does this mean you will keep me no matter how I falter or what I do? I know the answer is yes, because you made me a part of you!

HE WILL KEEP ME

There are times in our lives when things just don't seem right. Still I find me a place in the shelter of the Master's arms.

And He will keep me in the shadows of His wings. He will keep me under the protection of His care. Because I dwell in the house of the Lord most High. He's the Shepherd of my soul, He's my bread of life.

So when I can't find a friend and my strength is at the end, Jesus' love will be there. He's a good listener, He knows and He cares.

And He will keep me in the shadows of His wings. He will keep me under the protection of His care. Because I dwell in the house of the Lord most High. He's the Shepherd of my soul, He's my bread of life.

Now my life is in His hands, even before the world began. And I trust in His plans, for He's my Savior, my Lord, and my Friend.

And He will keep me in the shadows of His wings. He will keep me under the protection of His care. Because I dwell in the house of the Lord most High He's the Shepherd of my soul, He's my bread of life.

TAKE, EAT, THIS IS MY BODY

Jesus I can't see. You're no longer here in body. The truth is, I need to hold you. 'Take, eat, this is now my body.' I take in your word, like bread coming down from heaven! Your word gives me hope, thank you!

I know I have your word, but is it possible to feel your presence? Who am I to complain, when you went through so much pain? The least I can do is sacrifice, after you paid such a price. 'This is my blood. Drink all of it.' I drink in the warmth of your presence, of having you near. And like wine, your Spirit lifts my spirit and eases my mind.

It helps to know my labor is for someone that holds me dear.

CHANGING TIME

Betrayed and hurt, that's how I felt. I felt like I met my mate. I was making myself over, trying to please, and be received. My prayer was for confidence I would be myself. Even still I offered myself. I felt used and disrespected, yet I felt like maybe I deserved it. I felt like a fool, as if someone tore my clothes off and I enjoyed it. I didn't know how far my exposure would take me, how deep the hurt would go. I felt betrayed because I exposed myself willingly; and no one told me things would fold. Now I'm stuck with a love that won't die.

At times I feel totally ashamed of my feelings - feeling it's a sin for me to feel a certain way. The Lord allowed what appeared to be rejection, so I must be doing or feeling something wrong. At times I just ignore my fears, as long as I have something, anything to hold onto. Taking the mustard seed of faith given to me, I hold onto it for dear life. Still, I feel as if I can run into reality and my whole faith will shatter. So I stand still and wait, and I pray to God for the next season. Even when I pray, I feel at times I have faith, but no foundation, no reality, nothing I can put my hands on.

Part of me wants to open the door to unlock what's inside, but the thought of facing reality forces me to continue to hide. I try to find a friend, someone in whom I can confide. I wait for a sign, a listening ear but no one's there. It's not that they don't care, I realize they do, but for what I have to share I don't want it to appear new. So I look for someone with understanding. I don't want them surprised by what I release inside. Nor do I want to

be viewed by condemning peculiar eyes.
So I went to the Lord who knew and he cared. I opened the door and just stood there. I thanked and praised the Almighty and asked him to forgive me, then I released it all. Again I asked him for forgiveness, not for me, but for me to forgive those who trespassed against me. It was then he allowed me to see Genesis 2:25 and Genesis 3, and with this understanding he set me free:
There in the Garden of faith, standing as one, are the fruits of promise and vision. The desires of one's heart are promised realities. The vision is not depending on one's own insecurities. One must get out of the darkness and walk in God's light! Surrender one's own doubts and fears from toils and strife, and take a fruit from the Tree of Life. He changes opinions with His seeds of faith, by opening windows of understanding for life's circumstances through dreams. Prayer is the key for one to see and understand this spiritual manifestation. The challenge is not submitting to others opinions or fears exposing one to shame and self-condemnation. God's Holy Spirit reveals by revealing a better way. He convicts and transforms by clothing.

I can imagine the Lord saying, "How long will you seek my face, pondering my amazing grace? My unfolding love will shine on you, exposing the person you long to be. Willingly attached but surprisingly free.
I'll free you from the bondage of sin, and change you from within. Yes, with me, you'll be born again. I'll walk with you at our own special pace, as I take you to a higher place."

A FAITHFUL FRIEND

Everyone needs a faithful friend with whom they can tell their problems.

A faithful friend will take charge; he'll speak for you when times get hard.

A faithful friend will let you ride without experiencing abuse or fear as he drives.

A faithful friend will let you relax, and be yourself, without feeling pushed or pressured into being someone else.

A faithful friend is one in whom you can confide, and if you want to, hide.

LOVE REQUIRES

Light requires electricity, a battery, solar energy or some other source. Love is the same. It comes from a source other than us.

Love is a true confirmation there is a God. We drink from its cup, but we don't know its flavor.

Love breathes in patience and exhales understanding. The more patience shown, the more understanding received.

Love requires sacrifice: the greater the love, the greater the sacrifice. Anything less, do we not question it?

Don't limit love to a person, it could be something you love to do. Just stir up the gift hidden inside of you.

THE REASON FOR THE BATTLE

During war, it is important to have a secret place of refuge. Because war can separate a family, and sometimes separation is needed. However, every battle whether yours or not will affect your attitude. The biggest battles you will find are the ones in the mind. Just don't let it steal your chance to have life, for that is the reason for the battle.

HERE'S TO TOGETHERNESS

I long to hear your voice, to feel your touch, your warm embrace.

My eyes wait to see you, just to behold your face.

Soon we will come to meet, then we will taste goodness.

Our fantasies are our memories, where we savor each caress. Till we meet, here's to 'togetherness'.

MAKING A STAND

Trying to make a stand can be very hard to do when trying to prove that you're a man.

But a man, a real man should be independent. He should make his own footsteps that others can follow, not where his friends lead him. Sometimes a friend can be an enemy and that can be really hard. That's why a man's main concern should be between him and his God.

A true friend will always have an outstretched hand; he knows and he cares when you're trying to make your stand.

SHOPPING FOR ME

Thank you, Lord, for allowing me to see, I'm reaching for things that could actually be. You let me know you weren't rejecting me but, through life lessons, you were correcting me.

When my faith was shaken by circumstances around me, you let me know that you were preparing me. At first, I thought you were taking away all the things that were dear to me. Then I discovered you were emptying me of things that didn't belong to me. The doubts and fears that were on my shelf were from the outcome of someone else.

Now I stand with all my desires before me. And I'm not ashamed to say that I'm asking you for them. Sometimes I get nervous about you shopping for me. But I'm tired of guessing about how things should be, to later discover it's not working out for me. So I'm going to trust what you get will fit, and that I won't look like a misfit.

The beauty in this world is from the things (in nature) that stand. Likewise, Lord, help me to see the beauty in following you, as I put my shopping in your unchanging hand.

MY MAN TO BE

What Jesus is to me, that's what I want my man to be.

Jesus' love and kindness draws me, and causes me to submit.

With grace he tolerates me, as his unfolding love slowly fashions me.

When this kind of loving kindness is found in a mate, the grace in him will make me great!

THE SCARS OF THE PAST

Things will come up to catch you off guard. A rock in the road will leave a scar that changes you for life. As seasons pass, the scar will take its place beneath the skin. Remembering how it used to be at first, the scar won't seem too bad. But everyone who sees it remembers; so the memories and disfigurement never end.

You ever wonder if you journeyed to another place would it be the same. No one would know the story, but they would still see traces and want to know. Then the memories will play again.

Would the Lord be offended if you hid? Not who you are, but what you used to be. So you won't be handled as fragile with tender hands. The caution of others has an effect on the mind and what you are. It makes one feel as though he'll never be more than what he used to be.

Lord, forgive us if we camouflage the scars life's lessons left behind. We're not ignoring life's lessons; we're just forgetting some things, so that we can nurture who we are, and what we know we can be inside.

TRYING TO IGNORE

Trying to ignore the yearning in your heart to reach for more and be what you've always wanted to be.

Trying to ignore the yearning in your heart to reach for that dream love that will always cherish you.

Trying to ignore the yearning in your heart to unleash your feelings and really be set free.

Why do you try to ignore the yearning? Is it because you're stuck here in reality with challenges facing you?

While standing still, try praying to the Lord: He alone can change what you see with His words of prophecy.

I CALL HER MY GODMOTHER

I call her my Godmother, but she was a friend. She didn't mind revealing herself so that you wouldn't feel uncomfortable about revealing yourself. And when she gave advice, it wasn't a command; you could take it or leave it. She was a friend who *shared* with you, who took the time to have fun with you.

I call her my Godmother, but she was a teacher. She taught by example. She didn't mind working out the problem for you until you knew what you were doing. She committed herself, to show one how to be committed. She used her talents and gifts to impart to another person a talent. She was a mentor and a tutor.

I call her my Godmother, but she was a mother. She welcomed you as a gift from God. Yet, at the same time, she was a mother who didn't mind correcting you and asking you, 'Now what would Jesus do?' She didn't try to change you but rather she helped to develop you, to pull out the gift God invested in you. She was willing to nurture you, even if it meant carrying you, to show you the love of God. This demonstration of love overflowed even to the next generation.

I call her my Godmother, but she was a woman of God. She was willing to be whatever God needed her to be, whether teacher, singer, mother, father, comforter, or friend. She was a faithful servant, one in whom God could depend.

I call her my Godmother, but God called her His child. God's love is so great, that He continually gives to us people like Jesus, His

Child. For He promised not to leave us comfortless, though we experience grief for a while. So I end this poem surrendering, for just as *we* expect to be comforted, God must also comfort His child.
So when I called my Godmother, God called home His child.

AT A MOMENT LIKE THIS

At a moment like this, everyone dear and precious comes to mind. You don't want to think of any more tragedies.

Submitting to the sovereign will of God is always a sacrifice. Yet we know in our submission, that God, in love, is doing what is best for us. So we step out in faith, not looking at the circumstances, but to the God in whom we trust.

Though it seems hard for us to look past the flesh, God is not fashioning the flesh; He is fashioning the heart.

So at this moment, when the one so dear comes to mind, I remember it is not the tomb, to which He speaks life, but the one on the inside.

So God strengthen the inner man, like I know you can. You promised never to leave us or to put more on us than we can bear.

WHY DO YOU SEEK THE LIVING AS THE DEAD?

Why do you seek the living among the dead?

We came to lay spices on Him. We came to talk, and adore Him. Can't you see that we love Him? Who are these others? Do they even know Him? Are they angels? Are they messengers for Him? Why have they taken Him? Where has he gone?

Why are you weeping? Did I not tell you? Pain and suffering are a part of this body's destiny. But when I go to my Father, He will set the Spirit free. Don't cling to this body, it is just a shell. Don't cling to this building; it's just a space for the spirit to dwell.

Why are you still weeping? Did not you hear what was said? Why are you still weeping, as if I'm still dead? Don't cling to this body, it is just a shell. Don't cling to this building; it's just a space for the spirit to dwell. I must go to my Father, He's waiting for me. And when I go to my Father, I will have ultimate liberty!

You see, according to the enemy, death was meant to separate me. But now it draws me nearer, closer my God to thee!

IT'S OUT OF YOUR HANDS

We seem to endure many problems; and we try on our own to solve them. At night is the cry of endless complaints, even though the blessings we receive are too plain.

We testify, and call on God's name. We sing King Jesus. Is it all in vain?

If you call on Jesus, he'll be right there. Keep the faith and believe, he'll answer your prayer. If you want it, you can get it, but don't join the band. Just get on your knees because it's out of your hands!

WHAT ARE YOU TRYING TO PROVE?

I had a dream and, in my dream, I was looking at my watch and pondering how long before the Lord would make me one with my husband. Then my watch became a webpage. I was directed to a website titled 'The Way of the Master.' (In real life this website exists, but in the dream, it was given to let me know that this was the 'Way of the Master.') A man was speaking from Romans chapter 12 verses 1-3 (though he discussed Phil 4:13), and he said: Sure, we can do all things through Christ that strengthens us. We can step out any time we get ready; we have the Holy Ghost. We can work any job; we have the Holy Ghost. We can marry any person; we have the Holy Ghost. We can do it all, but that's a misinterpretation of scriptures. The object is not to prove that we have a testimony, the object is to prove the perfect will of God.

When we present ourselves as a living sacrifice, we don't choose the sacrifice, God does, nor is it our work, but God's. Sure, we can do many things. But are we moving when God tells us to move? Are we doing what God purposed for us to do? Are we with whom God purposed for us to be with? Are we fulfilling God's purpose, proving His will?

In other words, are we followers, learning from the leader or are we trailers, looking to see what our next course of action will be? Have we really learned to listen? If we are truly to be a body that is one and on one accord, we must first be on one accord with the Lord. We must realize that we are to conform to His Ways and transform to His thoughts. It is easy for us to think more of ourselves than we ought to when we think we are living a life that is pleasing.

Many times we do the work and ask the Lord to bless what we've planned and done. In doing so, are we asking God to conform to our ways and thoughts? Are we taking for granted the choices or commitments WE make, are the ones God purposed for us? Ask the LORD to give you a vision of where HE wants you to be, then ask Him to lead you. And make sure you follow!

I'M NERVOUS

I've never been this way before, I'm nervous.

I know the Lord is going to supply my needs. I know He's going to take care of me. But I don't know if I'm going to get what I want.

I've never been this way before, I'm nervous.

I've gone a new way before and I lost my way. I couldn't see straight and I lost my way. Now I'm weary of new ways.

I've never been this way before, I'm nervous.

I need your help. Order my steps, direct my path, and increase my faith. Let me know that you care about what I want, not just what I need. Sometimes it's hard for me to distinguish between the two. Obviously, if I need it, I would have it; because you would supply it.

I've never been this way before, and I'm nervous.

Lord, thank you for listening to me. Thank you for loving me, for always being there for me.

GOD YOU SEE ME

God I know you see me. You know how I feel.

Help me to see what you see. Help me be still.

I am torn; I don't know what to do. But you are all knowing; my help must come from you.

Help me Lord; I know you see me, tell me what I should do. I need your direction; and my heart needs your protection.

WHO TOLD YOU THAT YOU WERE NAKED DREAM

I was in a car and the Holy Spirit instructed me to take my hands off the steering wheel and drive under His leading and where He directs me. As I drove for a period of time with my hands off the wheel and cars driving quickly by me, I panicked and grabbed the steering wheel of the car. The Holy Spirit said, 'You ate ice.' I knew He meant that I failed to follow and trust Him completely. Then I decided I would try again. This time the car started swaying into another person's lane. Immediately I grabbed the steering wheel and said, "I'm sorry, I ate ice." Then the Spirit said 'Who told you, you ate ice?' Immediately my mind was taken back to the Garden of Eden when the Spirit asked Adam "Who told you, you were naked?" You see the first time I was instructed by the Spirit, or led by the Spirit, to take my hands off the steering wheel. The second time I decided to try on my own, though it was the same word, it was not under the direction of the Spirit.

Then it was revealed to me the difference between the sword of the Spirit (the word of God given to an individual by the Holy Spirit) and the sword of man (the word of God used by an individual but not by the leading of the Holy Spirit).

THE CALL, THE COST AND THE COMMISSION

God's Call to love is amazing! I am persuaded God allows love to penetrate so deep to cause surrender. It's the only way to endure the Cost. It makes you weak and vulnerable, but at the same time, it empowers you to press on. You feel bound but at the same time you feel liberated. And no matter how much I rant and rave, I've come to love the process.

My love has taught me so much. Being in love helps you to be kind, the trials help you to be compassionate and more understanding with others. When in love, attraction, just like the anointing, helps you compromise. No one has to force the other, all you need is a little time away; the anointed attraction (God sent love mixed with chemistry) will give you strength to stay. You'll want to know the other better so love can have his way.

Daughters of Eve, let me spare you, there is no microwave method for a change. No knowledge, message or reading can have your eyes opened like God's right away. A word from the Lord is like food being digested, it takes time to pour into the heart nutrients needed and filter out what doesn't belong. A Call or revelation is not a green light, no, but rather a red light. It is time to stop and listen, so you can answer. Yes, red lights can be nerve wrecking; sometimes the hardest thing to do is wait! But red lights allow others to pass by who aren't going your way; and it's okay because they won't get what you see.

And know this, every Call has a Cost, a proceed with caution, a sacrifice, a giving up of something, a setting apart, yes even a separation to learn what is required or expected going forward. But by the time you are Commissioned to go forward, you will fall in love with love and find confidence in God's plan.

LOVE'S SWING: I WANT TO KNOW YOU

I want to know your mind, to share in your thoughts. I want to know what runs across your mind, when that charming smile of yours is wrought. When your smile kisses your eyes, I want to see what you see.

I want to know, I want to know you.

I want to know your mind, to share in your thoughts. I want to be your friend, when life problems come down hard. When sorrow fills your eyes, I want to be your support.

I want to know, I want to know you.

I want to know your mind, to share in your thoughts. I want to know the hopes and dreams that you reach for in life. When they fall in your grasp, I want to be there by your side.

I want to know, I want to know you.

I want to know your mind, to share in your thoughts. I want to know the concerns you hold deep within your heart. When it's tenderness you need, I want to help give you peace.

I want to know you, I want to know you.

I want to see your smiling face, spend every minute in your embrace.

I want to know, I want to know, I want to know you. I want to know you. I want to know.

LOVE'S SWING THE GIFT OF LOVE

We come before your presence for a blessing. Thank you, Father, for the gift of your love.

We come before your presence for a blessing. Thank you, Father, for the gift of your love.

Provide us with strength to endure all things. Provide us with strength from your love.

Lord, provide us with patience for what we hope for. Provide us with patience from your love.

We come before your presence for a blessing. Thank you, Father, for the gift of your love.

We come before your presence for a blessing. Thank you, Father, for the gift of your love.

Provide us with faith that builds each other. Provide us with faith from your love.

Lord, provide us with joy when we're together. Provide us with joy from your love.

We come before your presence for a blessing. Thank you, Father, for the gift of your love.

We come before your presence for a blessing. Thank you, Father, for the gift of your love.

LOVE'S SWING: BLESSED BY HIM

Lord, I want to be blessed by him; I want to find rest with him. I want to be blessed by him.

As you lead I want to follow him, to trust and to honor him, take counsel and advice from him. I want to be blessed by him.

Lord, I want to be blessed by him; I want to find rest with him. I want to be blessed by him.

At times doubt comes in my mind but there's no other friend I'd rather find. The love of his is one of a kind. I want to be blessed by him.

Lord, I want to be blessed by him; I want to find rest with him. I want to be blessed by him.

Lord bless him to provide. Supply him with what he needs, so we both may live to enjoy our lives. I want to be blessed by him.

Lord, I want to be blessed by him; I want to find rest with him. I want to be blessed by him.

LOVE'S SWING: IT'S NOT JUST A FANTASY

It's not just a fantasy, when he touches me, for I can feel him inside of me, moving inside of me, and his love teaches me.

And he fills me up on the inside; He is my man, and I am his bride. And his love teaches me, how he wants me to please him, how he wants me to please him.

When I am lost, his meekness leads me; he makes me meek. And when I'm in doubt, with long-suffering he shows me patience, giving me faith, faith, faith to stand by his side.

And he fills me up on the inside; He is my man, and I am his bride. And his love teaches me, how he wants me to please him, how he wants me to please him.

When I am down, his good, his goodness consoles me, his goodness. And when I'm uneasy, his peace holds me, he gives me peace.

You see, you see, you'll see, it's not just a fantasy. It's not just a fantasy, it's not just a fantasy.

ALL OF ME

When he touches me and holds me, then I know why I could never give myself to another, because I've already given him all of me.

When he helps me with the smallest things, he reminds me I'm his queen. When he gets into my head to reach my heart, he reminds me he cares and I'm glad.

I desire to give more! Tell me what does it mean to give one's problems, fears, and dreams to another? Does my future become his?

When he touches me and holds me, then I know why I could never give myself to another, because I've already given him all of me.

TOGETHER AS ONE

When we said we'd be together, we became one.

Yes, God ordained the husband as the head, and the wife as his body.

Well after you get through using your 'head', see about me.

When you receive your knowledge, don't uncover my nakedness: cover me instead. Don't let the knowledge and strength you receive expose my weakness.

Make sure I'm washed, remove all doubts and insecurities.

Make sure I'm fed, give me the counseling and nurturing I need.

I'm a part of you. Look at me! Am I together? How am I dressed? It may cost a little something for me to look my best.

You have the eyes. If I've become weighed down by the things that I do, check to see if I should try something different, or something new.

Don't get upset if this becomes a routine, sometimes that's what it takes to lose excess weight.

Please watch how you carry yourself, for you carry me too. Don't be closed minded or withdrawn, you know how you think has an effect on me.

Yes I have a responsibility; I have to put on and absorb whatever you give me!!!!

I HAVE NOTHING

Having filled my head with nothing all day, I have nothing to offer. My brain needs stimulation, but I don't want to get it from a substance that leaves me useless. Lying around, taking in what this world has to offer on the media, I came up empty. Hanging out with others keeps my mind off the truth: I haven't reached my destiny.

But I thank God for heads! They help bring understanding to the scriptures that were read. Find a woman's story in the scriptures that didn't involve man, it will be a story so short, it was over before it began. Men receive revelations from the battles they go through, women, the story is explained to you. The battles men go through becomes the bread by which we are fed, as the Lord becomes the one in whom they confide. This unveiling changes our very lives. So I thank God for heads; they help bring understanding to the scriptures we read.

Now my whole body is looking to engage; I want to use all the talents and gifts God has given me. I was created to make God look glorious! One will never know how beautiful a story can be, until he or she has been loved unconditionally!

KNOW ME

Many who know me may be wondering, how can a single person, who is a virgin, write in such a way? Well God, who is the author of Love, subjected my heart (refer to poem, 'Subjected Heart'), but He also gave me a secret place (refer to poem, 'The Secret Place.') to write my story. So I felt love, rejection, and loss; but I also felt the comfort and hope that only the Blessed Hope can give. Was it just to share with others or is it a petition still to be answered? God knows, and my hope is built on the Love of God!

YOUR WILL, MY INHERITANCE

Lord let me cling to your Will for me. Let it never be said that my will superseded your Will for me; for I know your yoke is easy and your burdens are light.

Your Word is like rubies in a poor barren land. It uplifts my spirit and gives me strength to stand.

Your Love is like fine linen encompassing me with warmth and honor.

Your Will provides my every need. Help me to cling to your Will; for I know that your yoke is easy and your burdens are light.

Let it never be said that my will could ever supersede yours.

GIVE YOU THE PRAISE

Lord send your river of praise. Lord send your fire of praise. Lord send your river of praise.

Lord, I want to give you the praise. Help me give you the praise. Lord, I want to give you the praise.

Give me a vision, show me your hand, so I can see the joy in your plan and give you the praise.

Lord, I want to give you the praise. Help me give you the praise. Lord, I want to give you the praise.

Lord send your river of praise. Lord send your fire of praise. Lord send your river of praise.

Lord, I want to give you the praise. Help me give you the praise. Lord, I want to give you the praise.

Help to compel me, supply the love that I need, so I can value all your changes in me and give you the praise.

Lord, I want to give you the praise. Help me give you the praise. Lord, I want to give you the praise.

Jesus you're worthy, We give you the praise
Jesus you're worthy, We give you the praise
Jesus you're worthy, We give you the praise
Glory Hal-le-lu-iah, We give you the praise.

LIKE THE EVERGREEN

Make me like the Evergreen, able to stand in all kinds of weather.

It will not matter what comes my way, I will remain green forever.

As seasons come and go, somehow I will continue to grow.

Through spring, summer, fall or winter, my leaves wouldn't fall and my stand wouldn't wither. Of course I must agree, despite changes around me, to be what God created me to be.

AN OUTPOUR

This season is known for its outpour.

Born to fly, I appreciate my wings.

High above the clouds, I see nothing but beauty.

I'll tell you what I see: moist soil - good for digging, raised (uncovered) food - good for picking, broken trees - good for building, fresh water - good for cleansing.

I see a dam breaking like a water bag, disrupting homes causing labor pains. And I see new life, fresh starts, new jobs, and new homes - a season good for gathering.

DIFFERENT SEEDS

We got different seeds, everyone. We come to testify, tell of what He's done.
So let the praises ring, give Him everything, 'cause the whole world needs to know.
We got different seeds, everyone. We come to testify, tell of what He's done.
So let the praises ring, give Him everything; let the Lord God take control.
We got different seeds, everyone. We come to testify, tell of what He's done.
And we all got praises, we all got praises. We thank Him for the battles won.
We got different seeds, everyone.

AN EXAMPLE

I want to be an example of what Jesus means to me.

He died on a tree; so that I could be free. And that's what I want others to see.

I want them to see: freedom, from the bondage of sin. Freedom, to start all over again. Freedom, from the struggles within. Freedom, from the fear of death caused by sin.

Freedom, freedom!

I want to be an example of what Jesus means to me.

He died on a tree; so that I could be free. And that's what I want others to see.

I want them to see: liberty, free to have fellowship with God. liberty, free to sing praises to him. liberty, free to lift up my hands. liberty, free to come boldly to his throne. liberty, free to call heaven my home.

Liberty, liberty!

I want to be an example of what Jesus means to me.

He died on a tree; so that I could be free. And that's what I want others to see.

I want to speak liberty: to those dying in their sin, speak liberty, and tell them they can be born again, speak liberty, and tell them Jesus died for them, speak liberty, tell them happiness is with Him.

I want to speak liberty, liberty!

I want to be an example of what Jesus means to me.

He died on a tree; so that we could be free. And that's what

God wants others to see.

THE LIGHT OF MY LIFE

The beauty of your sunshine brightens up the day. I thought when the storms came it would chase you away; but the warmth from your sunlight burned through the trees, melting all the rain away.

Thank you for being the dawning of another day. You are our hope that troubles will soon go away. Thank you for your constant faith and abiding love; even in the midnight hour, you light our path. I thank you Lord, for your seasons are an extension of one long day. No matter what the situation, no matter what the season, the light you give is always there.

Your fall is like sunset; the falling leaves paint the land, like the sunset paints the sky its strange color. When the fall comes, it seems like we lose everything. But your rainbow of colors serves as a reminder that all will not be lost. Not even the summer months could bring out such beauty. Its beauty reminds us you're still there.

Your winter is like night; sometimes it's hard to feel your presence. At times a person can get cold feet. Even so, your snow is like moonlight, it lights up the path. The shimmering snow of winter helps the holidays glow.

Your spring is equally special, the showers are a sign of new beginnings. It's like the dawn of another sunny day, without it all hopes of growth would be washed way.

Your summer is sunshine at its best, melting away all the pains from yesterday, as you season us with growth.

THE LIGHTHOUSE DREAM

In the dream we were in lighthouses, and all that lie on the outside was darkness. The people on the outside were full of bitterness, accusations, and evil speaking. When things were put up to block the light from shining on the outside, it also darkened the house on the inside. Then the darkness from the outside would press against the house and affect our attitudes. When we let our light shine it hindered the darkness from coming into the house and affecting us on the inside. When we did not let our light shine, the people from the outside would affect our disposition and further hinder us from letting our light shine.

In the dream, I was showing this to a brother but it was too late; he was consumed by the darkness surrounding him. He was full of bitterness, accusations, and evil speaking.

WHAT MORE CAN I SAY

He gave me this world. What more can I say? He gave me the sun to brighten my day.

Everything green breaks forth with a dance. The flowers and the lilies lift up their hands.

When the beauty runs out, He lets them down gracefully. He paints their leaves, and gives life to their seeds.

I suspect he'll do the same for me! Why? Because he gave me this world. What more do I have to say?

THE GOD I CAN'T SEE

It's hard for me to figure out this God I can't see. But I want to go to Heaven and I heard He can take me. He left His Word to lead the way. But it's hard for me to understand His Word. I don't know what He's trying to say. Why does God have to be a ghost? Why hasn't he shown himself to me? Is he afraid of what I might see?

What's this? What's with this man on a tree? Suddenly I saw two strange images next to me. They handed me the book and said, 'Here, take a closer look'. Then I saw the man on the tree as a little boy like me. I followed his life from the pages in the book for this was someone I could see.

His parents didn't own him; he wasn't a piece of property. He listened, asked questions, and learned a trade. To the poor and homeless, he was King - his little became so much. To the outcast, rejected, and illegitimate steps, he was comforting. To the scorned, falsely accused, and misunderstood, he was a mentor. To those incarcerated and abused, he was more than a conqueror. To the physically challenged and challenged authorities, he was a redeemer. Now I can see God, the Word was made flesh, by a man I could see!!

THE OPPORTUNITY

A grandmother comes out of a house, made with molten clay on the sides with a cloth sheet draped on top, facing her grandson. She lays her hand on his chest, looks into his bright brown eyes, and turns him to her right, his left, saying, 'Go. Make something of yourself. You've been given this opportunity, take it.'

The grandson has on a blue dress shirt with a t-shirt underneath, black dress pants, and shoes. The grandmother has on a white scarf, a white blouse that hangs over her skirt, and sandals.

It is late in the afternoon, the sky is cloudy and bright. The boy has a decision to make, follow the family caravan on his right or the opportunity on the left. He responds, 'I want to, but the family needs my help.' The family is gathering alongside a cart, covered with a striped cloth, on wooden wheels attached to a horse.

The grandmother replies, 'You can help. I told you how. Pray. Now go on.'

The boy's youngest brother around eight years old runs up, dressed in a t-shirt, pants and sandals, and pleads with him saying, 'Don't leave me. Stay. Come with us.' Another brother, closer to the boy's age, comes in, looking at the boy's youngest brother and says, ‘It's time to go.’ All the brothers stare at each other waiting for the boy's response. The boy looks into his brothers’ eyes; it's like looking into his own. The boy makes his decision.

The caravan begins walking alongside the cart. There are six in the caravan, the father, two females, and three males. The Father leads the way, pulling the horse on the dirt road. The surrounding landscape is dry and barren. Every male has on a t-shirt with dark pants, a turban wrapped around their head and neck, and sandals. The females have on a blouse, a short wraparound skirt (for easy running), scarves on their heads and sandals.

The boy looks and feels like an outsider in his dress clothes. He slowly falls behind as the caravan moves forward. After a long while, the caravan comes to a place where there are a lot of high rocks proceeding upward on the left side, and isolated high rocks on the right side.

The Father stops the horse and says, 'Hunt.'

Immediately, everyone tries to grab a gun from the cart before the other person gets one. One of the females yells at the youngest saying, 'Hurry up brother.' Shots are fired. Everyone runs for cover behind rocks. Those who were able to grab guns continue to shoot at targets – each other!!

One boy, wearing a long striped robe, was not able to grab a gun before shots were fired. He was shot in the shoulder while running to get behind a high rock on the right. Leaning with his back against the rock, you can see the blood stain through the robe and his bright brown eyes as he cries, 'I've been shot!'

Tell me, is this your story? Are you the boy? Did you take the opportunity, or did your dreams die in that dry barren land?

THE BIRTH OF DEATH

I couldn't recall the day I was born, but I had seen birth. This seems pretty much the same.

Like a child at birth being pushed out of her mother's womb, I was being pushed out of the womb of life. I could feel this day coming. The pressure from life let me know that I couldn't stretch time out any further.

Leaving the comfort of life caused me to cry out. The separation sent chills through my body. The hospital room was my incubator.

The doctors knew, and so did I, that someday I would be moving on.

Like water in a freezer slowly changing to ice, I could feel my body growing cold as it adjusted to the new phase I was in.

Like a child at birth being pushed out of her mother's womb, I was being pushed out of the womb of life. I can't recall the day I died, but as for life, that was the end.

WHAT DO YOU THINK ABOUT?

What do you think about on the inside when you're looking on the outside? Do you cry? Do you smile? Do you think of a chance or a change?

Tell what do you think about when life's doors swing open, to reveal a mountain you must climb? Do you walk away? Do you grasp hold? Do you think of what might happen if you fall?

What is it that you think about? Is it the faith you need to remove your doubt?

What do you think about when you discover the problems you face are based on decisions you make? Do you make a path? Do you follow? Do you live in fear of making mistakes?

Tell me what do you think about when time is a toll, you face on the road? Do you spend? Do you save? Do you think of the price you must pay?

What is it that you think about? Is it the faith you need to remove your doubt? Tell me, what do you think about? Is it the faith you need to remove your doubt? Tell me, what do you think about? Only faith from God will bring you out.

TRUTH TO SHARE

There is a truth I need to share. The truth is this: God is always there.

There is a truth I need to share. The truth is this: God is always there.

And he will fight for you; he'll battle for you.

For he is our Shepherd, and he is our King.

There is a truth I need to share. This is the truth: God is always there.

CHRISTIAN EASTER RAP

Christ died on the cross for our sins.
Clap, Clap
But then He rose again,
Clap, Clap
with all power in His hands.
Clap, Clap
He got rid of His body,
to live in our bodies,
So we can rise again.
Clap, Clap

EPILOGUE

Thank you for scrolling through life's up and downs with me. I pray you find strength from whom I believe. This is my first book, but it won't be my last. If you want the melodies to some of the songs, give me time, it's coming along.

ABOUT THE AUTHOR

Kyra Haymon

Kyra loves writing, teaching, singing, and listening to audiobooks. She has been writing since she was 8 years old; however, this is her first book. Kyra was raised in a Pentecostal home. And though she speaks in an unknown language at times, she believes this book will speak to you.

www.ingramcontent.com/pod-product-compliance
Lightning Source LLC
La Vergne TN
LVHW090522110826
845146LV00003B/950

* 9 7 9 8 9 8 8 1 9 6 3 1 0 *